# FINDING
## YOUR
# PURPOSE

SARAH MARCELA

Trafford
PUBLISHING®    www.trafford.com
North America & international
toll-free: 1 888 232 4444 (USA & Canada)
fax: 812 355 4082

# *Dedication*

------◆❖◆------

I am blessed beyond measure to have many wonderful people in my life. Thank you all. You all have a special place in my heart to many names to mention. Praises to family for there love and support over the years. Shelia Thank you for all the dinner parties. Joanne for the Late nite phone calls and always being a Covenant sister.

My mom Gwendolyn who passed in 2005. For your love of family and unconditional love for me. You with God and Robert James Jr. my Father were would I be? My brothers each one of you have taught me that I am a jewel a diamond in the rough. I would not change you guys for nothing in the world. Bobby I often wondered how it would of been if you lived with us but God brought you in rite on time You taught me how to stay focused. My mother in law Sexy Zee I thank God for him placing you in my life cause he knew your personal testimony about family and friends. You have Taught me a whole lot about life and how to Win. Thank you for being a true friend you are a beautiful person let go and let God. Mama Nae I could not have wrote one word with out you and your prayers for me and my family. We love you much. All that wisdom late nite to early moring thank you for being a covenant sister.

My Husband for your steadfast love over these years. You are my best friend, the patience, understanding & compassion you expressed during this whole project enabled me to Prevseverse. Brandon Jr.(son) you were my inspiration to write this book listing to all my war stories as you grew up. Bottom line son you can Win with God all things are possible. Last but not least Brittany(daughter). Watching you grow up has touched my heart in so many ways you are little blessed stay in your word. You came to win your a little me just pray before you make decisions always put God first.

# *Introduction*

I have written this book with you in mind. My desire is that you will take some of these simple principles and actually apply them to your life.

I am sharing a few dynamics that have helped me overcome some challenges in my today, situations that occurred in my past had to be redirected so That I could win and have victory in my life.

My belief is that as I find solutions to life's real situations and circumstances I must share them with others. This book is my attempt to share those solutions in language and thought patterns for generations to come. These stories are trials over triumph. And broken down for the saved and unsaved because I have experienced both worlds.

When I began to write the manuscript I knew it that it would take more than natural ability so therefore I relied on the supernatural ability.

It is through this book that I realized the power of who's I am. And the message the message I was sent to deliver in these end times. To motivate people to live the best life possible to maximize the pain & hurt from there past relationships and move on. This book is for the person that was told they ain't never going to amount to nothing. This is for the drug addict that was told once a drug user always going to use drugs. The men &women that are in relationships that are a lie. Learning through this book that Only God can get into the middle of a Mess and make it a miracle. I hope that this book inspires you to trust God in all that you do.

# *Preface*

————◆◆◆————

I am BAD, Blessed And Delivered. That is what I am all about. You don't need a doctorate or a masters degree or any kind of formal education to be BAD. All you need to do for that is to accept the Good Lord into your life and think on the things He says. The Lord helped me to learn how to make it in this world; not only to stay on the right side of the law but to stay on the right side of Him. Because of this my husband and I have been able to live good, comfortable lives and to help other people as well.

In 1998, I received my Evangelism certificate, making me part of His alliance.

In 2003, I got my ministerial licence from Anointed by God's Seminary Alliance International, and I was ordained in 2006.

In 2008, I got my honorary doctorate in humanities for life experiences from that same seminary.

Now, I teach motivational improvement classes. And I teach Biblical Finances. Yes, Jesus told us everything we need to know about earning a good living and how to handle the money you do have, if only you would read and listen to His words.

Everything really comes down to remembering that we are all God's children, and we've got to treat each other right. Some people believe we are here on this earth, in order to learn how to behave. If that is what it is about, then the most important lesson for you to learn is; How do you take care of each other?

First, in order to take care of someone else, you have to learn how to take care of yourself. It is next to impossible to love anyone else if you don't also love yourself. Too many people have told you that you aren't worth anything and that there's no way you can ever amount to anything good. I'm writing to say that simply isn't so.

You need to understand that all the bad stories people have been telling you about your being worthless drug addicts and not intelligent are full of crock. If the only person around who can tell you a better story about yourself is you, then you need to go to God praying and weeping and praying and weeping some more, until you are able to laugh and tell yourself a better story than the one that you have been carrying around all this time.

I wish I could save the world from all the pain and suffering I see around me, but I can't. You have to learn to do what's right and help a body when God puts him there in front of you and you have the ability to do something to make his life better. It is up to you to grow a relationship with God so that you can grow a helpful and healing relationship with yourself. If you always tell yourself that you are wicked and evil and weak, then you are in a fair way to being wicked, and evil, and weak. It's up to you to put that old stuff away where it belongs—in the trash-heap. You may have to throw those bad stories away, over and over again, because those negative things we tell ourselves do like to trot themselves out, shake themselves off and dance up and down in front of us. The truth is; those bad stories are lies. Every one of them. After all, weren't we made in God's image? Isn't that one of the first things the Bible tells us, all the way back in Genesis 1:26-7? 1:26 goes something like this: And God said, "Let us make a human in our image, by our likeness, to hold sway over the fish of the sea and the fowl of the heavens and the cattle and the wild beasts and all the crawling things that crawl upon the earth. And 1:27 says:

> And God created the human in his image
> in the image of God He created him.
> Male and female he created them.[1]

In Acts of the New Testament, verse 17:29, doesn't it say; "Therefore, as God's offspring we have no need to imagine that the divine being is like a gold, silver or stone image, made by human skill and thought.[2] God does not have evil children. God does not have any children who cannot be redeemed to live a good life. God gave you the choice and the ability to get up every morning to get up and walk in the way of His light. Some days you may not do so well, but you pick yourself up, dust yourself off and get back on the good path.

After a while, it becomes distasteful to continuously do things that make you unhappy, or that make unnecessary trouble for the people you care about. That is one of the surest signs that God is helping you to be the person He meant you to be.

The reality is, you cannot sit around doing nothing about your life, expecting that everything you need will simply float down out of the sky exactly when you want it, the way you want it. The universe generally doesn't work that way. You have to get up off your butt and do the work that is in front of you. This is always the place to begin. You do the work in front of you, pray for guidance, and then you look around us to see how you can make things a little better for a few other people.

It's the junk and the baggage in your life that holds you back. Memories from your childhood of abusive parents who taught you to accept abuse from your spouses during your adult years. The mistakes and failures that pile up, leading you to believe that you can accomplish nothing good in this world. But, all those negative experiences could teach you, if you would open your heart to their messages. They teach you to be compassionate with yourself and with other people who are hurting. Some of the sages teach that after Christ was crucified he spent three days in Hell, before ascending to Heaven. That was to give him a true understanding of hopelessness, and to teach you that Jesus does care.

---

1    Robert Altar; The Five Books of Moses; W. W. Norton and Co. NY, London; 2004
2    Common English Bible

Mary Magdalene came to Jesus plagued with demons. Jesus freed her from those demons and then invited her to be one of his disciples. As Christ told the demons making misery of Mary Magdalene's life to go away, you need to tell those demons that are making you miserable that they don't have to stick around. They are free to go back to where they came from. You know what demons you have. How about those demons of self hate, or lust, or the demon who keeps telling you you're no good for anything? They just keep repeating the same things over and over again, because they can't change. The one who can change is you. How could it possibly be that you, who are all made in God's image, are no good for anything? You really do know better than that. Tell those demons they don't have to stick with you and that they are free to go away.

Everyone has made some whoppers of mistakes. Some of us have spent time in prison. Some of you have hurt people really bad. But the demons of self hate and the demon of hate against all the world, and the demon of guilt that won't even let you shake a leg in the morning when you get out of bed—tell them they don't need to hang around any more, cause you are following the path that Jesus makes for you.

You can learn from your mistakes. Sometimes it takes a terrible mistake to show you that you aren't paying good attention to what God is telling you. When the angel told the Prophet Elijah to, ". . . Go forth and stand upon the mount before the Lord," and behold the Lord passed by and a great and strong wind rent the mountains and brake in pieces the rocks before the Lord but the Lord was not in the wind. And after the wind, an earthquake, but the Lord was not in the earthquake. And after the earthquake, a fire, but the Lord was not in the fire. And after the fire, a still, small voice." [3]

The Old Testament was originally written in Hebrew. The Hebrew word for still is d'mamah, which also means gentle. God's voice is gentle and may come to you in the midst of turmoil when you are not listening for it.

So, you made some mistakes. So what? You pick yourself up, dust yourself off, assess the damage, make your atonement so that you are less likely to make the same mistake again. Then you shake your sins and demons from out of the corners of your clothes, and we move on with your life.

How do you go about doing this? The first thing is to sort out what is true and what is not. Sometimes all you can do is keep on praying and then pray some more, to find what is true. As it says in 1 Samual, 12:24 Only fear the Lord and serve Him in truth, for consider how greatly he has done for you.

The word for fear, yara in Hebrew, can also mean to honor and revere. And the word for truth, emet, can also mean firmness, faithfulness and reliability. The word for Great, gadol, can mean to grow up, or to be magnified. So, you must honor and revere the Lord and serve Him reliably. And you need to grow up. The more you do this, the easier it is to see what is true in your life, so that you can make meaningful changes.

My friends tell me, "You need to tell those girls that they can grow up to be anything they want." That is what this book is about.

---

[3]    First Kings 19:11-12 KJV

# *The Beginning*

---◇❈◇---

Genesis 1:1 ~ In the beginning, God created the Heaven and the Earth.

1:2 ~ And the earth was without form and void; and darkness was upon the face of the earth. And the spirit of God moved upon the face of the waters.

In Hebrew, which, as I said, is the language the old testament in our Bible is translated from, the description for the earth is tohu vavohu, which means both empty and turbulent. Even though there wasn't anything there, a lot was happening.

Most people, who meet me and see everything I have and what God has accomplished through me, don't believe me when I say that I had a difficult life. I was the youngest of six children, and the only girl. However, even though by the time I was born my family was pretty well off, my parents and my brothers had all experienced what it means to be really poor. When you are poor and Black, prejudice is insidious. You see it and feel it, everywhere you look.

My parents had been dirt poor before I was born. I used to hear stories about what went on during those years, but I never experienced the sort of poverty my brothers did when they were little. People who have to live through awful things because they are too poor to be able to do anything about them often wind up carrying a tremendous fear of poverty. It can be like having a monkey ride your back, goading you into doing crazy things so that you never have to be poor again.

By the time I was old enough to remember anything, we had plenty of money to spend, but a lot of it came from drugs. My daddy's sisters and brothers lived downstairs from us and they were into dealing big-time. They had cash spilling out of drawers and cupboards. I could go downstairs almost any time I wanted, grab handfuls of the stuff and head for the nearest department store to buy anything I wanted—and no one ever missed that money.

My father may have been involved in a few things that would raise some eyebrows in so-called polite society, but he believed strongly in those old—fashioned virtues known as respect and honor. I was about five or six years old when one of my older brothers, Jamar, robbed a bank. The police had not yet caught up with him, and he might have been able to get away with it if it hadn't been for my daddy.

Now, he had told Jamar, several times over, that he did not want him to bring any of his girlfriends into the house. I was little and my daddy did not want me to see people having sex. He believed that a child's innocence is precious and something to be guarded. I had a few other big brothers, but Daddy wouldn't let them live with us, so I did not get to know them well, at least not while I was little.

It was January—cold and snowy outside. My father happened to walk into his room and found Jamar in bed with a girl. I don't remember that daddy said much, but he burned with a white-hot anger. He ordered the girl out of the house immediately, just as she was—which happened to be naked. My father then called the police and told them the part my brother had played in the bank robbery. Naturally, they immediately came over to take him into custody. Snow was thick and deep outside, and it was cold. I saw the girl stumbling barefoot through the snow, trying—without any success—to hide her nakedness. My only thought was that she needed something to cover her herself with. I dashed back to my room, grabbed the sheet off my bed and ran out the door in my bedroom slippers and nightgown, clambering through snow that came up over my knees, with the sheet balled up in my arms, calling to her to stop so I could give it to her to wrap herself in. I must have been about five-years-old then. Years later, that woman came back to Alabama for my mother's funeral. She remembered me, even though I had long since forgotten her.

You might believe that I was so little then that losing Jamar to prison wasn't such a big deal. But Jamar had been a large piece of my life. Every time holidays came around, or my family did things together, all I wanted to do was cry, because Jamar wasn't there to share it with us.

The brothers I remember most from those years were Thomas and Davon. Thomas was the oldest and he was my mother's right-hand man because he took care of us when she had to work. He was steady and kind and he was the next one to go. For me, Thomas was the brother I looked up to and depended on. Davon was a couple of years younger than Thomas. He also looked up to his older brother, and tried to do everything Thomas did, though my mother seldom depended on him to carry responsibility as Thomas had always been the steady one.

My mother used to send us to schools outside our district, because she believed we would get a better education there than we would if we went to the schools near where we lived. We came from a pretty rough district in New York City, and I think she was right. Thomas did his best to take care of us while my mother and father worked, and both our parents did work long hours. My mother taught him how to comb the tangles out of my hair, and he used to do that for me every day. He also helped me with my homework and some nights he made supper for us. But what was most important, he and my brother Davon would guide me through the maze of city busses and subways every morning so I could get to the elementary school, before they went on to their high school. Every afternoon, he and my brother Davon would come get me at the elementary school, and we would repeat the process going home again.

We were all devout Five Percenters. This is a religious group that broke off from the Nation of Islam in 1964. The Nation of Islam had broken away from the Muslim faith several years before that. We used to call ourselves the Nation of

Gods and Earths. The movement started in Harlem when Clarence Smith began to teach a way of thinking and feeling about the world that is radically different from the Muslim faith. Up until 1964, Clarence had been a devout Muslim of the Nation of Islam. Clarence was a charismatic teacher, and he was able to convince many people that what he said was truth. He taught that God was the original Black man and that Earth, as the supporter of all life, was the original Black woman. He believed that people working together can create the energy that makes things happen on this earth. He taught about the Supreme Mathematics and the Supreme Alphabet. They were his way of associating numbers and letters with mystical meaning, something like the Jewish Kabala. He taught that the word Allah stands for man. His teachings helped a good many people believe that they could finally get up off their knees to accomplish good things with their lives.

But for the Muslims, Allah is one—there is no other god but Allah, and the Nation of Islam, which is another Black version of the Muslim religion, said that the Five Percenters were heretics. Those schisms, those—what should only have been petty disagreements—became gang warfare. Of course, nearly all the boys in inner-city New York wind up joining one gang or another, whether they want to or not, especially if they are black. For a young boy growing up in those neighborhoods, joining a gang is as quick and easy as stepping out the front door of the house.

We were all strong believers in what the Nation of Gods and Earths taught. I spent hours studying the Supreme Mathematics, and I am certain that my brothers learned to have a sense of themselves as being able to make good changes in this world. But—and there always is a but—other people were afraid. If Black men truly saw themselves as gods, they could become powerful enough to make real changes in society. That would surely change the status quo, so it had to be stopped. Kids in the other Muslim gangs started attacking my brother Thomas with knives and chains, so he took to carrying a gun around with him. Angry kids who have nothing better to do than attack each other will sooner or later make big trouble. The sat part of it is, they haven't figured out that attacking each other only makes things worse. They should be using all their wonderful energy to find good ways to change their lives.

A lot of people believe they can feel when changes are about to happen in their lives, such as when someone will be badly hurt, or when a terrible accident will occur. But for most of us, such changes come as a shock. It was fall, just beginning to get cold. I had to get up early so that Thomas and Davon could get me to school and still be able to get the subway that would get them to the high school in time for their first period classes.

Thomas was looking worried. Davon tried to crack a joke about some young gang member looking pretty sloppy. Thomas sat beside me, silent and grim-faced, staring out the window. I knew he was packing a gun, but I didn't want to think about why he needed to keep a gun with him. He was just Thomas, my big brother who was always there when I needed him.

I will probably never really know what happened to Thomas in school that day. All I knew was that he and Davon did not come for me when school was over. They had never even been late before. Sometimes I would dawdle, gathering up my books and papers, gabbing with the other kids, and my brothers would be waiting for me in the office wondering what had kept me for so long. However, on this day they were not there. When I got down to the office, the two secretaries were sitting out front at their desks, talking back and forth about someone who had been shot at the high school that day. No one said a word to me—I might as well have been invisible. I was too shy to ask whether it was Thomas who had been shot. He had been acting like he knew someone would attack him, even though the last thing he wanted people to know about him was that he was afraid. All I could think was that my favorite brother was in the hospital. He might even be dead the way those two women were talking. I sat on the bench waiting for my brothers and getting more scared with each passing moment.

And then Nettie Beverly walked in the door. She stopped at the front desk to tell the secretary that she had come to take me home. Nettie Beverly is one of my father's cousins, and back then she worked as an aid in the school cafeteria. She must have been about twenty-five-years-old. I always thought she was a beautiful woman. She was tall and slender, and she wore round prescription lenses and had a gold tooth that glinted when she smiled.

You better believe that by the time she walked in, I was so full of questions I was ready to burst. I have always liked to talk. Words spill out of my mouth without provocation. Some people say that one of the hardest things to do is to get me to stop talking. But I knew enough then not to make a scene and not to be disrespectful to my elders. I just bit hard on my tongue, crossed my fingers and prayed that my brothers were all right. I followed Nettie Beverly out to the parking lot and climbed into the car beside her. I didn't dare open my mouth till she had turned the ignition on. "Is Thomas OK? Was he shot? Is he dead?"

Nettie rolled her eyes at me and slowly backed her car out of the parking lot. "No, dear. He's OK."

That was the last thing she said about him till we got to her house and my dad came to take me home. I didn't learn about who had shot whom, or what it was about, until the two of them started talking about it. I had been sitting in the kitchen with a glass of milk and a chocolate chip cookie when my dad walked in.

He sat down out in the living room with Nettie and I could hear bits of their conversation. "Shit. Virginia's going to be so angry when she hears about this."

"You haven't told her?"

"No. I happened to be at home when the police called and told me to come down to the station. I didn't get to see him for a couple of hours, even then—not till after they handed me a ream of papers to fill out. Then they only let me see him for ten minutes."

Police? Thomas was being held at the police station? I put down my glass of milk and hunkered down as still and quiet as I could behind the door. If I walked into the livingroom and asked questions they would both stop talking, and I wanted to learn everything I could before they did that. When Nettie Beverly spoke again her voice cracked, like she was trying to hold back a sob. "He was always such a good boy. I'll talk with the pastor of my church. A lot of folks there know him."

My dad's voice always got really husky when he was upset. "His mother always thought he'd be a lawyer. Heck! Thomas wanted to study law. There ain't no law school's gonna take him now."

"Yeah. Shooting someone in school is guaranteed to ruin everything."

So, Thomas had shot someone and he was going to be in jail. I couldn't stop myself from running out to the living room with tears streaming down my face. "Is Thomas ever coming home again? Will I ever see him again?"

Nettie Beverly handed me a Kleenex and held me tight. "Course you're going to see him again. Some day."

I didn't know what to think. Almost everyone I knew had a brother or a cousin who was in prison, or at least had been on the wrong side of the law in one way or another. But my brothers were part of my home. Even if I did get pretty annoyed with them for teasing me, they were my brothers. It took a while to sink in that I might not see Thomas again for a long time. I didn't realize then that prison is a pretty lousy place to grow up.

Nettie Beverly took me to and from school every day from that time on. Davon would ride with me on the bus to her house, and Nettie would take me through the bus system on to school.

I learned a lot about what it means to be a good person from her. She was one of the people who opened my eyes to what Jesus' message can mean. Nettie Beverly didn't earn a lot of money as a school cafeteria aid, and she worked hard for what she did get. But she loved God and she was married to a decent God-loving man who backed Nettie when she felt the spirit telling her to give. Every so often someone she knew would go through a time of particular need, and she would slip a hundred dollars into their pocket or hand bag when they weren't looking. For years, nobody in her church knew who was giving the money away just when they needed it most. Nettie Beverly was one of those people who found joy and fulfilment in helping those around her in whatever ways she could. She was not a big talker, but her words tended to be wise. She served on the board of her church for many years and she was one of my better angels.

Thomas was booked for shooting that kid at the high school and sentenced to serve twenty years at the state penitentiary in Elmira, New York. The shooting had been part of one of the gang fights. The Nation of Islam kids were out to get rid of the Five Percenters. Thomas was not the type of guy to pick a fight, but he wouldn't back down from one either. He had been good to a lot of people, and everyone who knew him knew he was intelligent and honorable and ambitious. Nearly everyone in Nettie Beverly's church and most of the Five Percenters wrote letters of character reference to the judge, so his sentence was commuted to five years of prison with ten years of parole. He served those five years by working hard at being a model prisoner. Whatever he saw and whatever he had to do in prison, his desire to be honorable and righteous came through somewhat intact. But his having to leave home left me feeling like my right-hand man had been taken away. There were times when I felt as though he might as well be dead. He wasn't there to crack a joke and he wasn't there to protect me.

My father used to work in the construction business, and on weekends he ran a gambling casino. So, once Thomas was in prison, my parents had to depend on someone else to take care of me. For a few years, this was a friend of theirs named Mary. She used to work at the same nursing home that my mother did. Mary always treated me as though I were her own daughter. She did have a girl, Pamela, who was about four years older than me. My folks used to pay Mary well to take care of me—well enough that she bought a four poster bed for me to sleep in while I was there on weekends, just like the bed Pamela had. She enrolled me in the Sunbeam Children's Choir at her church, and bought fancy dresses for me to wear. Between what Mary was teaching me on weekends and what Nettie Beverly had to say to me on the way to and from school, I had a real taste of what it could mean to worship Jesus.

My life was full, but I felt empty inside with both Thomas and Jamar gone, making it a whole lot easier for me to get into trouble. And growing up Black in New York City means that trouble is everywhere. It's almost as though people expect you to get into trouble, and they aren't happy until you've gotten yourself into a mess with the law, or wrecked your life with drugs. Even with my aunt Nettie and Mother's friend Mary taking care of me every day, trouble was right around the corner from where I lived. It was walking down the halls at school and standing on every street corner.

For me, trouble began in the form of a gang of kids that called themselves the PHO. They were pretty well organized. Someone had found sweaters that you could order with your initials on the front and the big PHO across the back, all done up in bright colors. All of us who could afford to bought one of those sweaters and proudly wore it to school every day. I can see you reading this and smiling and saying, there's nothing wrong with wearing a bright colored sweater to school. All the athletic teams have sweaters, and some of the other clubs around school have one too.

No, the trouble part was because we weren't really trying to do anybody any good. We were trying to protect ourselves from the other gangs, and if you're young and living in the city, you almost have to join a gang if you want to stay alive. That's how rough it can be out on the streets. So, belonging to the PHO was sort of like protection for me, after my brothers were sent up. Other kids used to be afraid of us. Some of the guys who belonged to the PHO were the toughest guys in our neighborhood. We were also one of the most popular gangs in our school. Everybody who wasn't afraid of us wanted to join up with us.

We often used to leave school early in order to go to someone's house and take drugs. I don't think we started out with the hard drugs. There was a lot of pot. The thing about pot is that even though it's harmless, you can't shake off the feeling that you are on the wrong side of the law for smoking it. We also did harder drugs—heroin and other stuff like that. Those are drugs that can do more real damage to your mind and body than most kids even want to think about.

My life at that time was an interesting mix. In the morning, Nettie Beverly would help me get to school, and on the way she would be telling me to trust in Jesus. On the weekends, Mary would have me, and every Sunday she dressed me up to go to church. There I would sing hymns of heavenly praise in the choir. But during the week, I was exploring what was out there with my friends and all of us were pretty mixed up.

We felt like we were immortal, even though we'd all seen guys we knew die in gang fights. We were all thinking—it won't be me. It's always the other fellow who gets hurt or dies from this. It'll never be me.

One of the Five Percenter Elders had given me the name of Princess Talkisah. I liked that name and I spent a lot of time trying to find the princess within. I studied the Supreme mathematics and the religion until I was fourteen and I met Keith, or Mr. Perfect, as he was known among the Five Percenters. He reminded me of my brothers—fast with the women and out to make a buck any way he could without stopping to think who might be hurt.

The age of thirteen is a turning point for most kids. They aren't children any more and our society isn't ready to accept them as adults. A thirteen-year—old kid's mind is not the trusting mind of a child, even though he knows next to nothing about life. A thirteen-year-old kid's mind is opening up and suddenly he is able to reason and analyze on a level that he never has before. He's brand new at this activity, which is why he feels as though he knows everything better than any of the adults around him. The truth is he doesn't know didly-squat about life.

Every girl who saw Keith wanted him. He was hot good looking. He could have been a model in GQ, or some of the other classy mens magazines, but I don't know if that sort of thing had ever occurred to him. He knew that all he had to do was walk into a room and half the women in it would be drooling and the other half would be clawing their way over to rip his clothes off. At that rate, he had no reason in the world to be faithful to any one woman or girl.

When he started hanging around with me, I thought it was the greatest thing that could have happened. Keith and I were hot and heavy for each other right from the start. At least, I was hot for him. And Keith? I'm not sure even now what he was hot for. Sometimes I look back on what we were doing then and I feel as though he was trying to get me addicted to drugs, because he knew my family had money and big-time connections to drugs. It looks to me as though he thought that if I got into drugs to the extent that he was, that he would be in with my family— some of my cousins who were really making money selling them.

In a way, I was really lucky back then. Drugs were still only a game for me. I tried some of this and a little of that, along with the rest of my friends, but I never craved drugs to the point that I was sick if I couldn't get any. So, I thought I could walk through life experimenting with drugs and the heavy ones wouldn't really hurt me. Maybe I was wise enough to know when I'd had enough, or maybe I just didn't like the feeling of being high well enough to let myself get addicted to them the way some of my friends did.

There was one thing I did do, and I could have done that very easily without drugs. I got pregnant. By the time I was fourteen I'd already had three abortions. I was nowhere near ready to be a mother and Keith wasn't the marrying kind of guy. Each time this happened, all I wanted to do was get rid of the fetus and go back to seeing Keith again. So, I used to beg my daddy to take me down to the clinic so that I could get an abortion and he took me, even though I'm sure it broke his heart to see me living so recklessly.

My mother had told me many times that Keith was nothing but bad news. My brothers had seen him around and knew what kind of worm that kid could be. They got together a few times and beat him up to make him stay away. When I said my brothers beat Keith up—well, one night they pistol whipped him and another time—it was Easter Sunday—they attacked him with a hot iron. I was a fourteen-year-old kid and I knew less than nothing except that I wasn't ready to be a mother and Keith wasn't ready to be a good daddy to any kids. But I was so high on hormones that all I could think of was being with him. It could be that if I had chosen to keep those babies my parents would have helped me take care of them. Maybe if I'd had the courage to keep the first baby I would have understood what a jerk Keith was being a lot sooner and I would have been contented to let him go. The crazy thing was, I never asked my parents if they would help me that way, and they never told me that would do that. All I knew was that I surely wasn't ready to be anybody's mother. But if my brothers were going to be so dead set against him seeing me, and both my mother and my dad would have done anything to keep me away from him, then of course I'd have to find ways to see him. I chased after him because my brothers were beating him up and because my mother and father had nothing good to say about him. Back then, I didn't need any better reason than that.

Verse 7:3 in Exodus says, But I will harden Pharaoh's heart that I may multiply my signs and wonders in the land of Egypt.[4] This verse is part of a very confusing story. Why would God harden Pharaoh's heart in the first place? Moses was trying to get the Jews safely out of Egypt. He was doing everything God told him to do to get that done. He'd been to Pharaoh several times saying, "Let my people go." And each time Pharaoh put up another road block so that the Jews couldn't leave Egypt.

Now, God could have softened Pharaoh's heart. He has the power to do that, just as God could have softened my heart, back when I was rebelling against everything anyone tried to tell me. But, God chose to harden Pharaoh's heart that I may multiply My signs and My wonders in the land of Egypt. In Hebrew, the language the Old Testament was first written in, Egypt is called Mytsrayim. This word means narrow and constricted. It was as though I was in a narrow and constricted place then, and my heart was hardened to everything people who loved me tried to tell me. God wanted even the Egyptians to understand that He was more powerful than any of the gods they had been worshiping, so He hardened Pharaoh's heart on purpose so that he could send the plagues down on Egypt—all ten of them.

Now, what I experienced wasn't exactly the ten plagues described in Exodus, but I did have to struggle through a heap of trouble so that I would learn to recognize God's signs and wonders.

But you see, I had just come into my ability to reason, and I didn't know the first thing about life. Besides, hormones were a whole new experience and I was addicted to them far more than I ever would be to any drugs. And because I'd only just discovered hormones, I felt as though not one of the adults I knew could possibly understand what I was feeling. So, what did everybody telling me to stay away from Keith do? What did all their lectures and their best intentions

4    New American Standard Bible

do? Of course I knew what I was doing. After all, wasn't Keith Mr. Perfect among the Five Percenters? And why would I want to give him up when every other girl I knew wanted to have him? My mother got so upset over the situation she went to Jamaica. So it was my daddy and me, and he stood by me through that time.

A good trait, a very good trait, something we all could use more of—the will not to let anything stop me from doing what I had to do—got turned and twisted into a very wrong direction. We've got to have determination to see things through. If you have set yourself a goal, and you know in your heart and soul that it is the right goal for you, then you cannot afford to let anyone stop you from achieving it. It is not only your right, but it is your duty to God and yourself to make sure it happens. And like the teenage kid who will dare to crawl under and climb over any restrictions put in her way, you have got to learn to see your way around and through and over restrictions and roadblocks put in your way, when you know that what you are doing is right and worth achieving.

All through my childhood my daddy had tried to protect me from the rough and sordid side of life that was going on all around us, but when Thomas was sent off to prison—Thomas, who had been among the kindest and steadiest boys I'd ever known and who represented stability in my life in a way that nobody else even came close to doing, because everyone else was too busy making money—when Thomas was sent to prison, I stopped caring about being good. Thomas had been good, and look what happened to him. Working hard to be good just didn't make sense to me then.

# The Belly of the Whale

Jonah 1:1 ~ Now, the word of the Lord came unto the son of Amittai, saying;

1:2 ~ Arise, go to Nineveh; that great city, and cry against it, for their wickedness is come up before me.

1:3 ~ But Jonah rose up to flee unto Tarshish, from the presence of the Lord, and went down to Joppa, and found a ship going to Tarshish: So, he paid the fare thereof, and went down into it, to go with them unto Tarshish, from the presence of the Lord.

1:4 ~ But the Lord sent out a great wind into the sea, and there was a mighty tempest in the sea, so that the ship was like to be broken.

1:5 ~ Then the mariners were afraid, and cried every man unto his god, and cast forth the waves that were in the ship into the sea, to lighten it of them. But Jonah was gone down into the sides of the ship, and he lay and was fast asleep.

1:6 ~ So, the ship-master came to him and said unto him; What meanest thou, o sleeper. Arise, call upon thy God, if so be that God will think upon us, that we perish not.

I didn't have to look for trouble, it found me. All I had to do was go outside and walk around. Because so many young black brothers can't get a decent job because, a lot of them turn to dealing drugs. There were more drug houses down my street than you'd realize if you didn't know the people living there. Selling drugs was the only way a lot of us were able to afford the nice looking homes we had. Unfortunately, with the hard drugs comes addiction and with addiction comes violence, especially when large sums of money are involved. The real truth is, poverty is one of the ten plagues. It can make you powerless, in a world where power is everything. You could say that addiction to drugs is another plague.

So, as I say, trouble was waiting on the front doorstep every time I went out. It always had been out there, but until then, I had been able to avoid the worst of it. Or maybe it was more like trouble hadn't paid any attention to me. The thing that had changed for me inside was that I didn't care about being good any more. I had built a wall around my heart in order to shield it from any more pain, and I didn't care about what any of the good people who loved me had to say, or even what the good book had to say.

###

My brother Davon did the best he could for me. He helped me get to and from our cousin Nettie Beverly's house every day and picking up some of the slack around the house after Thomas left. But two years later when he was only sixteen-years-old, he got an eighteen-year-old girl by the name of Donna pregnant. I'm not sure what Davon was thinking at the time. He had always looked up to Thomas and now Thomas was serving time. He had literally thrown his life away when he was sixteen. At least, that's the way some people saw it. It may be that getting that girl pregnant was Davon's way of throwing his life away too, a way that he could still be like his brother. Or, it could be that Davon thought he could marry into money, or that love would save him. At the age of sixteen, it is not likely that he understood what it means to love a woman. However, Davon must have been hurting as bad as I was, and simply doing what he thought he could to fill that empty space inside him. Besides, sixteen-year-old boys are plagued with more hormones than a saint would know what to do with.

Davon's girlfriend had some money of her own. There is a story behind this, but you'll find everything has a story if you do a little digging. The actress, Stephanie Mills, had been doing a show in Covent Gardens. Thousands of people had come to see this show. She had brought a troop of performing horses with her, and they somehow got loose. A few hundred people were badly trampled, and Donna was among them. Her arm was broken and her skull was crushed in the melee. She had plastic surgery, but her arm was always deformed after that. Her family sued Stephanie Mills, and won a few million dollars from the insurance company, enough that their daughter could live comfortably on the interest from that money for a number of years.

By the time Davon met her, she had practically given up any ideas of getting an education, or running a business, or anything else that might have given her life a direction. She figured that with all the money she had, she already had everything. She had her own car, bought fancy clothes and ate at expensive restaurants whenever she wanted. She even had her own apartment. The only thing she didn't have was someone to love her. Davon could be decent, steady and caring, when he wasn't going wild on drugs. She figured she could buy him the way she had bought nearly everything else for the past few of years, and Davon thought he would let her.

Once she knew she was pregnant with Davon's baby, she insisted she would keep the child even if, ". . . I have to live in a tree and nurse it myself!"

My family wasn't about to push her to give the baby up, and apparently her family felt the same way. So, Davon pretty much moved in with her. He wasn't ready to be a daddy at the age of sixteen, though he did love that baby. Even Davon says that it was the swank clothes, the car and being able to go to fancy places that made him stay with that girl for as long as he did. Within a year, he got another girl pregnant. He may have liked being with the second girl more than he did with the first one, but the first one kept dangling her money in front of his face, and back he would trot to her. Davon has learned a few things since, but it took him a while. Sometimes I wonder if he ever did learn how to love a woman, but that is another story. He also spent a good part of his life in prison and that never does a man any good.

Thomas had just got out of prison. I was fourteen and he was twenty—one. He had tried to be his best while he was in prison. But you have to remember that everything that is done in prison is calculated to tear the prisoners down and to destroy any sense of self-worth they may have had before they were sent up. Law enforcement in the US calls anyone who makes a mistake or breaks the law a bad guy. In their eyes, no matter what a bad guy does, he's still a bad guy. Policemen aren't above telling lies in order to make sure those people they are calling bad guys go to prison.

We all thought and hoped and prayed that Thomas would pull himself together and make good when he got out of prison. I don't agree with everything Thomas says and does, but when he makes up his mind to do something, there is no stopping him. We thought that just maybe he'd figure out how to build a life for himself. He still had girl friends everywhere he went, and he'd never had to learn how to be faithful to any one woman, because he could easily draw women to him.

Once he and Davon saw that beating Keith up didn't keep me away from that guy, they decided to move down to Tennessee to be with one of Thomas' many women friends. I think Thomas wanted to be as far away as he could get from anything that reminded him of what had put him in prison, and Davon wanted to be with his brother again. That rich girl was beginning to wear thin as far as Davon was concerned, so going down to Tennessee with Thomas seemed like a pretty good deal. A cousin of ours by the name of G-Ball, who was into big-time drug dealing, drove down from New York City in his truck, to visit with them.

I'm not entirely sure what really happened. They may have decided to go with him on a deal—there are things about that time I will probably never know. What I do know of it is a story as old as time. The woman down in Tennessee found out about Thomas' girlfriend in New York. Maybe the girl in New York had tried to call Thomas and the woman in Tennessee had answered the phone. Maybe there had been a letter. Maybe Thomas talked in his sleep or called the Tennessee woman by the wrong name when he made love to her. At any rate, she burned with jealousy. She also knew that Thomas and Davon and G-Ball were headed up to New York City where that other girl was. She didn't want Thomas going anywhere or talking to anyone—especially if the place was New York and the person was young and female. Now the thing about jealousy and anger is they inspire the recipient, to get stubborn. Thomas might have liked the New York girl better, or he might have liked the Tennessee woman better, or he might have thought he could keep both of them happy, if only the Tennessee woman would shut up. Thomas and Davon and G-Ball were on their way back up to New York, and that fact was stuck in the Tennessee woman's head and wouldn't let her rest.

When jealousy attacks some people, they go crazy. They begin to figure that if they cannot have the man or woman they want—if he or she will not give him all his attention—then maybe they should just kill that person so that nobody can have him. This was the state of mind the Tennessee woman was in when she called the police to tell them Thomas had beaten her up and he was on his way up to New York, and wouldn't they please stop him from going there? She didn't know but she thought there might be drugs and guns involved. With the news that there were three young black guys in a truck that might be carrying drugs and guns, of course the police stopped them.

Many people don't understand how it can be that when work that pays a decent wage is largely unavailable, crime flourishes. G-Ball didn't want to be bothered with the nickle and dime jobs available to most black men in this country, serving time in Walmart or McDonalds and not making enough to get to and from work, let alone live. He had some cocaine in the trunk of his car and a handgun under the front seat. When you're involved in certain lines of business and certain parts of town, it's not safe to go out without a weapon. G-Ball was driving down the highway like anyone else. Davon and Thomas were riding along talking about who knows what—girlfriends, maybe. Keeping them all in order takes a bit of doing when you've got more than your share.

Thomas was a strong-willed young man when he got out of jail that first time, at the age of twenty-one. He still believed in those things he'd learned as a Five Percenter, things like honor and integrity. Davon always did want to live up to the standards his older brother had set. Neither Thomas, Davon nor G-ball, as we called him, would confess to owning either the cocaine or the gun and Thomas refused to rat on his cousin. Davon followed Thomas' example and wouldn't say a word. Sometimes when guys think they are being brave they are really being fools. The three of them were each sent up to prison for twenty years. Their lawyer insisted that if any one of them confessed, or told who it was put the gun and the drugs in the car, his sentence would be reduced. Not one of those boys would do that. They each spent fifteen years in prison, and they were middle-aged men by the time they came out.

I couldn't have kept quiet like that. My brothers had to do everything they were told, while they were in there, or things would have been much harder for them. But they were good, model prisoners. They arranged for family get-togethers and religious services while they were locked up. They won't talk much about what went on all those years. I'm sure there's plenty of stuff from that time that they would rather forget, if they could.

I nearly died that year—twice in one week. With Thomas sent up for the second time. This time, Davon was with him. I stopped caring at all about what could happen to me. Drug houses were pretty common where I lived. As I said before, my aunts and uncles kept one right downstairs from us. I knew where a number of drug houses were, and I knew a lot of the folks who ran them. I was pretty young and innocent, because I didn't know the kind of trouble I could land in if I spent much time in those places. My mother thought that if I came home every night around sundown, I'd be pretty safe—at least she hoped it would work out that way. But during the day, I went everywhere and did everything. Still, I was home every night for supper.

I was hanging out at this drug house in the middle of the afternoon. Nothing much was happening there. There was one guy I was sort of friends with, but at that time, the only thing I really knew about drugs was that some people made a lot of money selling them. And yes, I knew they were illegal. But my notion of what the law was and was not was pretty skewed. The guy I'd come to see was talking on the phone with someone, and didn't have time to hang out with me. It was a hot day, and I was getting thirsty, so I went down the street to get a soda. I hadn't been gone more than five minutes, when someone drove by in an elegant black limo and shot up everyone in that house. I heard the gunshots. Most people in that neighborhood did everything they could to stay out of sight whenever anyone went crazy with guns. I was about the only one who ran out to see what was happening.

I had never seen a dead body before, but there were three of them in the living room when I stepped inside the house. I must have called out—screamed—shouted—but no one answered. I turned around and dashed out the door, slamming it shut behind me and started running. I might have thrown up on the sidewalk, my sneakers smelled like I'd stepped in it when I got home, but I didn't care about that at all. I ran upstairs and hid under the bed. I stayed there for three days. I didn't want to see anyone or talk to anyone. One of those guys in the living room, half on the couch, half on the floor, his chest a bloody mess and his eyes and mouth wide open as though he was still shocked even after he was dead, had been my friend. I shrieked for several hours, till I became feverish. I didn't want to eat and I surely couldn't sleep.

After three days, youth took over. I had to get up and go out, just to see what I'd been missing. I called Petrie, one of my girlfriends, and told her about the shooting. She said she'd be right over. I knew a lady by the name of Pearl, who we could talk to.

Pearl had a nice place, and my girlfriend must have had a good talk with her. As it turned out, that lady was a drug dealer. It must have been a handy way for her to supplement her income. I saw a baggy of white powder stuff lying on the floor behind the coffee table, like it had fallen there by accident. I picked it up, went upstairs and rolled a joint with that powder. My girlfriend told me that she and the lady found me about half an hour later. They said I wasn't breathing and that they couldn't find a pulse, so they called an ambulance. There was that brilliant white light everyone talks about. Pearl didn't want any of the authorities to know what sort of stuff went on in her home. But when they could not wake me up, and it didn't look like I was breathing, Petrie insisted on getting me to the hospital. I even had an out of body experience like the ones people talk about having when they die. When I awoke, the doctor gave me a lecture. He said that when I arrived at the hospital, I was clinically dead. He said I had better get my life together, because the next time I did anything like that, they might not be able to pull me back. I learned later that, even with all the fancy equipment they have in most city hospitals, ninety-nine out of a hundred people who code die.

What I didn't know when I rolled that joint, was that the little baggy I had found casually lying on the floor held about $500 worth of uncut heroin, enough to kill an elephant. I began to feel as though maybe there was a good reason for me to be on this earth, though it took a few years for me to figure out what to do about it.

I saw violence up close and in your face that I hope my kids never have to see. I even spent some time in jail when I was a teenager. But this is not a story about how strange my life was, though I have seen plenty of troubles. It's a story about making a spiritual connection. It doesn't matter what names you have for God and Jesus. What does matter is how you connect with God. I pulled myself together enough to visit my brothers. It was a four or five hour drive, just to get to the prison where they were held. A dear friend of mine drove me back and forth, just so I could see them. A lot of good people told me I should stay away from them, but I insisted that they needed to know I cared about them. However too often, guys who have spent years in prison wind up opening up their anger on the people who went to visit them regularly.

For too many of us, living just this side of the law with one foot in prison becomes a way of life that must be unlearned before any other way of living can be learned. It couldn't have been more than a year after Thomas and Davon were sent up that I got involved with a Jamaican guy about twenty years older than me. It was about 1981. Sometimes it seemed like guys were selling cocaine and ecstacy from nearly every other house in the neighborhood. The police had a pretty good idea what was going on, and they worked to convict as many people as they could of selling them. They sent under-cover agents around to buy and sell drugs. They planted evidence where there hadn't been any, just to make a conviction. I wasn't even there when they raided the house my Jamaican frined lived in, though I had spent a lot of time hanging out there. I was walking over with a piece of whisky cake that my mother had made. In fact when the police arrested me, I was standing in front of the apartment building that I now own. They took me down to the precinct and showed me gun cases filled with high powered guns, which they said they had found in the drug house. If they were showing me real evidence, that house had been armed as though the people there intended to go to war. They told me they were filing five A-1 felonies against me, enough to put me away for fifteen to twenty-five years. When they told me I should call my parents, I was too afraid to do that. "I won't call my dad, cause he'll kill me." At the time, I thought I was being funny, but I really was afraid of what my father might do. I called my mother's youngest sister and her husband Lamont, and they came down to the precinct. I kept telling the police that I had never seen the cocaine and the guns they were showing me and that was the truth. The police said I had sold 500 grams of cocaine to an undercover agent. They said there were 550 vials of crack and they wanted me to confess to having sold it. All I knew to do was tell the truth—I had never seen the stuff before.

Diane and Sharon, a couple of friends of mine who were several years older than me, each did sixteen years as a result of that raid. Diane told me I should play insane—that I had got involved with those guys because I was crazy and didn't know what I was doing. I didn't want to pretend I was insane. I was only sixteen, so I thought they would only send me to juvenile. But instead, they sent me to Rikers Island, the prison of legend. Full lock-down. The most humiliating experience for me was having to take off all my clothes and squat and cough in front of the female guards. I wanted to cry, but I would not let those guards see me do that. "But I didn't do it—I'm innocent!"

The guards weren't all unsympathetic, but they'd seen it all. "Yeah, that's what they all say."

Right from the start, I was fuming about the rules. The first day I was in the cell block, I saw one of my cousins. She told me not to tell anyone that I knew her or that she was family. What I didn't understand was that it was against the rules for family members to fraternize. All I knew was that I was lost and very frightened. I called my mother and cried on the phone for about half an hour, weeping because my cousin would not let me speak with her. My cousin was in the same cell block with me and I wasn't even supposed to act as though I knew her. She was right, but no one told me how the rules worked until it was too late. By the end of the day, the guards had sent her off to another prison.

There was a girl in there known as Big Bad Pam. She was in the adolescent division with me and she used to sit on the phone all night. For whatever reason the guards didn't stop her from hogging the phone. Maybe they did it on purpose to make all the other girls in there as angry as they could be. I tried to call my mother one day and Pam hung up the phone on me. She stood more than a foot taller than me, but I figured I couldn't afford to back down. It was either her or me. I beat her hard on the head with the phone receiver and wrapped the cord tight around her neck. Two officers marched out of what they call the bubble, a protected area surrounded with bullet-proof glass where the guards hang out and see everything going on. They handcuffed me and marched me down to solitary, or the hole as we called it. I spent sixty days in there. When you are in solitary, you are not permitted to talk to anyone, and you are only allowed out for about an hour each day, to take a shower and things like that. They keep a guard posted at the door to watch and make certain the inmate doesn't try to kill herself and they pass meals through a grill in the door. No one spoke to me all the while I was in there. I could talk, I could sing and I could shout and pace back and forth. But you do get awfully tired of the sound of you own voice when there is no one around to respond. The sight of those four blank, gunmetal-gray walls staring back at you for hour after hour with no change and no let-up, would drive anyone nutty. I began to think I was hearing voices. The only book they let me read was the Bible. I read that book from cover to cover, and then I read it through again. Then I started talking to God. I was certain He was in that little room with me. Psalm 130 made a pretty deep impression on me then. Here is one translation:

> From the depths I called you, Lord.
> Master, hear my voice.
> May your ears listen close to the voice of my plea,
> Were you, O Yah, to watch for wrongs,
> Master, who could endure?
> For forgiveness is Yours,
> So that You may be feared.
> I hoped for the Lord, my being hoped,
> and for His word I waited.
> My being for the Master—
> More than the dawn-watchers watch for the dawn,

Wait, O Israel, for the Lord,
for with the Lord is steadfast kindness,
And great redemption is with Him.
And he will redeem Israel for all its wrongs.[5]

Thomas somehow found a lawyer for me, even though he was in prison at the time. The officers used to let me out of solitary to talk with that lawyer. He was a kind black man. He tried to joke me out of being so desperate and he told me to calm down. He said they couldn't charge me on the basis of the evidence they had, but they could say I was part of a conspiracy. My aunt told me to read Psalm 35, the one we call the Lord's prayer for legal counsel. That's the one that begins, Plead my cause, O Lord, with them that strive with me; fight against them that fight against me.[6] I read that psalm over and over again, and I am dead-certain that God answered my prayer.

When I came back out of the hole, Big Bad Pam didn't give me any more trouble, and I made friends with a girl named Suzette Williams. She was a lot like me and we used to talk constantly. She had been to a party where she got drunk and angry and cut another girl. She pleaded guilty to injuring the girl and got five years. When her parents came to see her, she would call me out so that I could visit too, and I would do the same for her when my folks came to visit. Even though I didn't know her folks and they didn't know me, it was a chance for me to talk with someone who wasn't a guard or another prisoner. I had to make nice to the guards even when I was afraid of them and the prisoners were often more insane than I was over having to spend years in an institution that is out to beat your spirit down. Any visits at all with someone from the outside are extremely important to a prisoner, because inside, it can be worse than being treated like an animal in a zoo. Visitors help remind a body that there is another world out there, and maybe a better way to think and to see things. I am not certain at this time what happened to Suzette after she got out of prison.

It was seventeen of the longest months I'd ever lived through, before the court got around to give me a hearing. Those were months I have always tried to deny ever happened. I spent years telling myself that, No, I wasn't in prison that long. It was only three or four months. Eight months? No. I wasn't there that long. But, I turned sixteen in February, and I was arrested in April. My hearing didn't come till August the year I was seventeen. Your sense of time does weird things when the reality around you is too harsh to accept. Your mind keeps trying to tell you that it isn't really happening, or that you haven't been there that long. You might say that time collapsed like a telescope, because your mind stops counting the days turning to weeks, turning to months and months becoming more than a year—all those months and weeks made up of one iron gray day after another, world without end. Get up when you are told, eat what they give you, stay out of fights if you can, but every hour of every day, you had better be ready to defend yourself, to stay alive. And every hour and every minute, you have to work not to let despair kill you.

---

5    Robert Altar; translation - The Book of Psalms
6    King James Bible

You can learn how to live in nearly any hell, maybe even beat the devil at his own game a few times, unless despair has over-run your heart and you let yourself believe that nothing is ever going to get better, and God is either too busy, or too far away, or maybe He isn't strong enough to answer your prayers. Or maybe, He just doesn't care. We have all had dark times in our lives, when the world around us looked as bleak as it could possibly be and all our prayers felt like they were going nowhere, or if our prayers were getting answered, they weren't the answers we wanted. It's times like that when you need to hunker down and keep on praying, so that every moment of every day, from the time you roll out of your bunk in the morning and put your shoes on, till the time you crawl back into it at night becomes a prayer.

Even in our darkest times, God is with us, all around us, playing hide—and—seek. You may feel like you have searched high and low and God wasn't there. But He is, and you will find Him. Perhaps, as the old story in Exodus goes, when God hardened Pharaoh's heart on purpose, so that when he worked His signs and wonders, Pharaoh and all his followers would worship God. It may be that he had to harden my heart for a while, so that I would recognize His signs and wonders in my life, and they would mean something to me.

When my hearing finally did roll around, my lawyer instructed me to plead innocent to the charges laid against me and the judge stipulated that I should go to a residential facility for drug rehabilitation. Even with my lawyer and my father there to stand by me, facing the opposing lawyer in that courtroom was devastating. Lawyers are trained to rip into every word a witness has to say and turn it around to make him look as though he not only committed that crime but a dozen others as well. That lawyer did a pretty good job of making it sound as though if the state didn't keep me locked up for the rest of my life, society would always be in danger from what I might do. I couldn't lash out at that lawyer, the way I had at Big Bad Pam, when he brought up all the evidence the police had fabricated against me, and presented it to the judge as though it was gospel. Even things I had said in the police station when they first brought me in he turned around to make me sound like a drug addicted, homicidal maniac. All I could do was try my darndest to keep cool. There were plenty of times in that courtroom when it was all I could do to keep from breaking down and crying like a little kid. But, as with all bad things, they do eventually come to an end.

I was never really addicted to drugs, they were just always around and I'd experimented with them, mostly when I was with Keith, not really understanding what those drugs could do to me, or what the legal system could do to me if I did not get those drugs out of my life. My lawyer concentrated on proving there was no evidence I could have sold all the drugs the police under-cover agent said I had, and I should have felt lucky when the judge said I should do thirty-six months at a residential drug treatment program, less the seventeen months I had already done at Rikers Island. And he gave the stipulation that if I had to appear before him again, he would make sure I got a five to fifteen year prison sentence.

I will never forget the day I was released from prison. When it was finally time I could leave, I came out that door and fell down on the hard, dusty sidewalk and kissed it—I was that thankful to be out of there and back in the real world. One of the guards who was escorting me asked if I didn't want to go back to get the clothes and stuff I'd had when I was put in prison.

"No way! I'm not going back in there ever again. Not for anything. You hear?"

# Returning and Learning

Jonah 2:1 ~ Then Jonah prayed unto the Lord his God out of the fishe's belly.

2:2 ~ And said, I cried by reason of mine affliction unto the Lord, and he heard me; Out of the belly of hell cried I, and thou heardest my voice.

2:3 ~ For thou hadst cast me into the deep, in the midst of the seas; and the floods compassed me about: all thy billows and thy waves passed over me.

2:4 ~ Then I said, I am cast out of they sight. Yet I will look again toward thy holly temple.

2:5 ~ The waters compassed me about, even to the soul, the depth closed me round about, the weeds were wrapped about my head.

2:6 ~ I went down to the bottom of the mountain. The earth, with her bars was about me forever, yet hast thou brought up my life from corruption, O Lord, my God.

2:7 ~ When my soul fainted within me, my prayer came unto thee, into thine holly temple.

I was allowed to go home for only one night. My father had found a place for me at Phoenix House, and I would have to go there the next morning. One thing I think of when I think of my mother is her wonderful cooking. I might have been hurt and angry sometimes that she wasn't there much, and that she seldom had time to talk, but she knew how to make a superb meal. Though after more than a year of prison fare, probably anything in the world would have tasted like heaven. I didn't know whether I felt like celebrating that night or not. I had no idea what kind of place Phoenix House was and there wasn't anyone I could trust who could tell me. At least I could take some of my clothes with me. Beyond that, all I could think was that this was going to be a lot like prison, or reform school or something, and I was really angry. One good thing about being so angry over my situation was that, more than anything else, I wanted to stay clear of all the guys who could ever get me in trouble with the law again.

Still, anyone who has problems with being told when and where they should sleep and when they should get up, Phoenix House could easily feel like prison. I didn't want to be there. I never had felt as though I had been addicted to drugs and I didn't believe I needed counseling for that. I had never experienced the Dts, or any of the hard-core cravings that make too many other kids too sick to be able to put their lives together. In my neighborhood, drugs were out there all the time. Even the harmless ones, like Dope, can get you into more trouble with the law than they are worth. For the rest, as I said, I had been able to experiment and come out the other side, without any of the physical cravings that make them so bad. And I always thought I could continue to experiment with them, at least sometimes. Being put in this place where the counselors made a point of telling me every day that I needed to stay away from substances that I didn't like much was about as maddening as it could get. All I really wanted to do was get out of there and get back home, where at least I felt as though I could have my own way. But the law said I couldn't leave. So there I was, stuck. Maybe Phoenix House was good for me. It was a safer place than most to get over my anger and learn what self discipline means.

1 Chronicles 13:11 says; When I was a child, I spoke as a child, I understood as a child, I thought as a child. But when I became a man I put away childish things. I began to grow up when I was in Phoenix House. I learned what it means to take responsibility for what I do and don't do with my life. Growing up and doing the best you can to be responsible for meeting your needs and help other people is one of the best ways there is to praise God. It's all part of being accountable for what you do.

Sure, I may have been safer at Phoenix House than I would have been roaming around loose, but I'd never really felt unsafe. Until I'd been sent up to Riker's Island, all the bad things had happened to other people, not me. Riker's Island shook me up. The result was that I was angry, like a cornered wolf, ready to strike out at anybody who even looked as though they could hurt me.

As soon as I got to Phoenix House and the counselor showed me where I would be sleeping, I was determined to take care of myself in all the ways that I hadn't been able to while I was in prison. In prison I'd had to wear the clothes they issued me—some sort of orange jump-suit. Orange is a hard color to wear all the time if you don't like it. At least at the Phoenix House, I could wear the clothes I liked. I'd gathered up some of my favorite things from home, stashed them in a couple of suitcases and now that I knew where my room was going to be, I wanted to iron some of my things so they would look sharp. Even if I couldn't be at home to sleep in my own bed, and hang out with my friends and eat any of my mother's fine cooking, I was at least going to look as smart as I could.

One of the counselors told me where I could find an iron and an ironing board and I set them up in the common room and started pressing my clothes. The iron was nice and hot when this girl came up to me. She might have been my size, or she might have been bigger, I don't even remember any more. She started shouting at me, "You can't do your ironing in here!"

I didn't say anything. I just held that hot iron up close to her face and she backed right down. I was one hot and angry kid. I had learned a lot about fighting and next to nothing about keeping my temper cool during my time at Riker's Island. The people at Phoenix House seemed to understand where I was coming from. They didn't treat me like I was in jail, they treated me like I was a real person. However it took me a while to understand that the counselors there really were interested in helping me to get a grip on my life.

Phoenix House had its own school for the kids who were there. In a way, it was good to be away from the public school, with all the gangs and the kids who were being tough because they had to be that way in order to survive, though I didn't think so at the time. A lot of teachers in the public schools treat black kids as though they were some sort of sub-human species; not capable of learning and not worth teaching. Even when a black student was putting out the best work he could, teachers in the public schools too often act as though it wouldn't be worth while to help a colored child—or any child who comes from an impoverished home—get a scholarship because, "He wouldn't know what to do with one anyway."

None of these things were true at the Phoenix House. There the teachers treated us as though we were worth teaching. I remember Linda, a science teacher there who believed so strongly in what she was doing that she inspired me, a hard-boiled kid fresh out of prison, to like science. Anyone who can do that is a good teacher.

God showed me the man who would be my husband while I was at the Phoenix House. When we were at home, we had only lived a few miles away from each other, but I don't think we had ever seen each other before we were both in Phoenix House. We didn't go to the same school, and he didn't hang around with the same gangs my brothers knew. This was probably a good thing. For reasons I am not likely ever to know, he decided I was the most important thing in his life. God made him love me. I had no idea of this till one afternoon I was late getting back there from a nurse's aid class I was taking. It was raining out and I was bounding over the puddles, trying to keep from getting too wet. There he was sitting on the front doorstep, weeping. He had been afraid something awful had happened to me. I looked at him and I thought, Oh man, I don't even know if I like this guy.

When I met him, Brandon was big. He was also strong and gentle and kind. But the first thing I saw was that he was big. Now, you might ask, if Brandon was so gentle and kind, what was he doing in a place like Phoenix House? He was in there because trouble met him on his doorstep as soon as he left his parents' home in the morning to go to school. It stalked him in the halls when he changed classes and it followed him home at night, like a wolf tracking its prey. As a result, he wound up in Phoenix House, only a few weeks before I would be leaving. They said he was in there for messing with stolen cars. Mostly he was there because he got involved with the wrong people at the wrong time. In addition to the cars, he got messed up with drugs, like a lot of black kids do, especially when their lives look hopeless. When he was sixteen he had a job with the Brooklyn Development Center—not a bad place for a sixteen-year-old boy to be working. He was living with his mother at the time and he managed to save a lot of money. Well, when his problem with drugs came up, his mother managed to get him into Phoenix House, and that is how we met.

Every day for the next week I tried to avoid him, but Brandon stayed by me anyway. He got along great with my mother and I don't think my father hated him. As far as my mother was concerned, Brandon was the son she always wanted. She took him fishing with her. She took him to Jamaica to learn about the cooking there. She took him to Europe to learn more about cooking. I might have been jealous that she didn't take me with her on those trips. She had taken me to Jamaica once when I was twelve-years-old and too young to be able to appreciate what she was showing me. But my mother and Brandon were buddies right from the start.

He certainly did grow on me. All those old songs like, "You made me love you—I didn't want to do it, I didn't want to do it," and "I grew accustomed to his face . . ." began to make sense to me and I didn't even listen to that kind of music. Over time I came to see that he, as in Ephesians 5:33 loved me as he loved himself, and I came to care about him more deeply than anyone I had known before. I wanted to be like the virtuous woman spoken of in Proverbs 12:4, who is as a crown for her husband. I awakened to God in about the same way I awakened to the man who would be my husband, bit-by-bit, one day at a time.

I studied and passed my GED when I was seventeen, while living in Phoenix House. After that, I signed up for some classes to learn to be a nurse's aid. I really wanted to be an LPN like my mother had been. It looked to me at the time like she had earned a lot of money working as a practical nurse, and I thought I'd like to take care of people the way she had. But my parents were earning too much money at the time for me to be able to get loans to go to nursing school, but they did not have enough to be able to pay the tuition for me to attend a school of nursing. Such are the joys of coming from a family that has a little money.

Because it looked like I was doing everything I could to attend all the classes, my social worker thought taking the nurse's aid training was a really fine thing for me to do. It showed I had some sense of ambition and that I knew I could do some good things. This was one of the first things that happened as I learned how to be responsible for myself. She had been giving me a lot of encouragement and treating me as though I was special. I think that meant more to me than almost anything she could have said by itself. She used to take me out to eat and to her home, just to visit and talk. I know that social workers are usually told not to get into personal relationships with their clients, as this could lead to dangerous situations, or simply heartbreak. But when someone like that treats a young woman who has been in trouble like a worthwhile human being, it can make all the difference in the world to her. If you are trying to help someone, getting in there and really being with her may be the best way to do it. I felt as though she liked me a lot. She saw all the work I was doing to pull my life together. I did everything God told me to do, and I did the very best I could. All that time I listened, and listened real hard, to that still, small voice within. She took me before the judge, a few months before I would have got out of Phoenix House anyway. That frightened me, for hadn't he said that if he saw me in his courtroom again he would have me locked up for the next fifteen years? But she knew what she was doing, even if I was scared. She took me back to get my sentence shortened, so that I would not have to stay in Phoenix House any longer. I had been there for fourteen months, so letting my social worker take me to court at the time knocked three months off of my sentence at Phoenix House. Being on trial the first time had been a walk through hell, and if my social worker hadn't been so sure of what she was doing, I would much rather have just served those last three months, thank you very much, than face that judge again. But she was right. I had been doing well, so I did get to go home a little earlier than I might have. For all my fear, that second court appearance was not nearly as bad as I thought it would be. The judge commuted my sentence, or whatever the word for that is, and told me I could live at home while I continued to attend classes.

I was looking forward to getting back to my mother's cooking and seeing my daddy again. But, moving back home wasn't as easy as I thought it would be. My mother's younger sister was in trouble. Her husband, who used to be a producer for Motown Records, had died. Suddenly she went from driving around in a great big pink Cadillac and having no worries about money, to having nothing. She lost her home because she hadn't paid the back taxes. Her accountant had always made sure things like that got done, but she had to let him go because she had no money to pay him. She had never understood how to save money, and she didn't understand how necessary it is to pay your bills. Aunt Rose and her husband had thought nothing of spending thousands of dollars on fancy clothes that they might wear once or twice in ten years, and she had never had to work at anything that resembled a steady job. Almost from the day she was first married, everything that she wanted had been handed to her. When her husband died, the money dried up. My aunt lost everything; her home and all that was in it, her car and even the friends she'd had before her husband died. She had no idea what she could do to earn a living. She had a nervous breakdown. I'm not sure where she was when my mother found her, but she was not in good shape. Of course my mother took her in and my father made sure she had a comfortable place to live and food to eat until she pulled herself together and figured out what she would do next. There was no way my parents would even dream of letting Aunt Rose live on the street. I came home from Phoenix House to find this aunt camped in my bedroom. It was one of the nicer rooms in the house and she wanted it, so she thought she should have it. She expected that I would let her stay there indefinitely and that I wouldn't put up a fight. Now, I know that in some homes, the children are expected to defer to their elders in all things. Ths may or may not be a good practice. I do believe that at least sometimes, this does teach the children that they do not deserve to have any of the nicer things in life. I chose to stand up to my aunt and neither my mother or father stopped me from doing that. "Listen, you don't live here. This is my parents' house and my room." It took her a while to see the light, but I did get my room back, and I helped her move all her stuff into the guest room.

This is as good a place as any to talk about books like The Secret that tell you all you need to do is think about something being there and it will be. It's called the power of positive attraction. There is some truth to this, but making things come your way by dreaming that you already have them is definitely not the whole story. Thinking, dreaming and believing that God is always with you and wanting you to have everything you need is one thing. Prayer is wonderful. God is Spirit, indefinable and everywhere. WE are God's eyes, His ears, His nose, His hands and His feet. We have to listen to what God tells us and then we have to do the work to make it so.

There is a difference between belief that is delusional, and belief that carries you forward because you know in your heart and soul that you are doing what God wants you to do. It is learning to do what God wants me to do that has made it possible for me to lead such a comfortable life now. Does that sound too simple, like some kind of hocus pocus? Well, it isn't. Sometimes it feels like the hardest thing in the world to figure out what God wants me to do.

The Quakers and the Jews speak of listening for the still, small voice within that tells you when you are doing the right thing. I listen for that voice and I read the scriptures and I pray. It is true for all of us, when you are following the path God wants you to, every day teaches you something you will need to know for that next step in your life.

Now that I was home from Phoenix House, I began to make trips to see my brothers in prison and I continued to see them nearly every visiting day for the next fifteen years until they were free. They were in there for a long time. I was thirty-one years old and they were middle-aged men by the time they got out. I had only been in jail for about a year and a half, but it was long enough to know how important it is to have regular visits from people who care what happens to you, even if they cannot do much to help you. I was determined to show my brothers that I cared. Sometimes, after I had traveled hours to see them, my brothers would be surly—really angry about all the horrible stuff they had to put up with. But talking wouldn't make the pain go away, so they never talked much about it. All they could do was keep on making nice to the man in charge and all I could do was go in every time I had a chance and tell them I loved them and I always would. I believed it was important to keep on telling them that, because when someone is in prison, whether it is a man or a woman, all his friends tend to forget he exists. It is as though he died, only worse.

People warned me that I shouldn't go see my brothers while they were in prison. People like the minister at the church where I went told me that once my brothers were out they wouldn't want to see me again, they would be that angry. Or, maybe seeing me would remind them of the time they had spent in prison, and they would want to forget that, if they could. That minister was right. Once my brothers were out, they didn't want anything to do with seeing me. I don't believe they really hated me, but sometimes they surely did act that way.

It is a hard call, and maybe there aren't any good answers to whether you should put a lot of energy into visiting someone you care about who is in prison. I know from my own experience that I really needed people to come see me, so that I wouldn't forget that life wasn't all gun-metal gray walls and less than friendly prison guards. But, on the other hand you cannot expect that your visits, no matter how regular and caring you are, will make that person be your friend when he comes out.

In the meantime, I was living at home with my mother and father and Aunt Rose. I finished the Nurse's Aid course and got a job with a telemarketing company. The work wasn't the greatest, but I did OK. People said I had a gift for selling stuff. I saved most of the money I earned, and that was really good.

There was a Nurse's Agency down the block from where my parents lived. That was where I had taken the nurse's aid course. Everyone there loved me, I suppose because I was ready to do anything and I had a lot of energy. But I think the real reason was that I was eager to learn what God wants of me. The agency sent me to learn the Red Cross first aid and CPR, which is how to resuscitate someone when they have died. They also taught me how to give meds in a hospital or nursing home, and had me certified to draw blood. They did this for me because the more things I could be certified to do, the higher my rate of pay would be when I went out on the job. I did some home health care work for this agency and the first three people they sent me out to take care of died. One elderly lady had given me the money to go get her groceries. I went to the nearest grocery store and bought everything she had told me to get and when I came back to her house, she was lying on the floor—dead. That's enough to make anyone wonder whether home health care is really what they want to do. But this agency was really good to me and I stayed with them. They sent me up to the Long Island Jewish Hospital. One of my patients there was an old gentleman whose legs had been amputated because of diabetes. He came to trust that I would be there when I said I would and that I would take good care of him. Even when the hospital assigned me to work on a different floor, I went back to see him every day just to make sure he was all right. He and his wife were both in their nineties and they were some of the best looking people I had ever seen who were that old.

When I worked at that hospital I made about eight hundred dollars every other week. He was ready to be discharged to go home, but he and his wife wanted to make sure that he would still get good care even though he wasn't in the hospital. He said that if I would come work for him, he would double my salary. I thought he was joking. Not many people can afford to pay someone eight hundred dollars every week. But the old man and his wife insisted they would pay me twice as much as the hospital was paying me. I showed them one of my pay stubs and they said yes, they could pay me twice what I had been earning. So, I went to work for them. They were really a nice couple. Their children had set up a separate apartment for the old man so that he could comfortably get the care he needed. Watching the two of them together, I learned what it can mean to be married. They had been together since they were both very young and instead of finding ways to cheat on each other the way I have seen so many married couples do, or being just plain nasty to each other, they did what they could to be good to each other and they both appreciated what they did for each other. His wife, who was on the far side of ninety, wanted to be the one who took care of her husband, even though he was heavy for her to lift and role from side to side and cooking was no longer easy for her to do. I learned a lot about what it can mean to love someone and some wonderful ways to show someone you love him, from watching that elderly couple be together.

They made sure that I had all the equipment I would need to be able to take good care of the old man—the lifts, the wheelchairs, and all that stuff. These were expensive things, but they bought that equipment so that I would not get hurt lifting him out of bed and getting him bathed and dressed every day. I used to take him out for walks every day that the weather was fine and they really appreciated everything I did for him.

These people even helped me get a car, so that I could get to their home quickly in case there was an emergency. I had been going back and forth on the busses, and that took at least an hour each way. I used to be at their home when I said I would be, but they were right, if they needed me right away, I would not have been able to get there in less than an hour. So, they told me I could pick out a car, and they would match me on the money I spent on it. My dad went to a car auction with me and we picked out a nice little car. The old couple's family—Zillo was their name—paid for half of it, as they said they would.

I learned how important saving money was, first from seeing how my aunt Rose lost everything because she believed she would never have to get off the gravy-train. When her husband worked with Motown Records, he earned more money than a lot of people ever see in their entire lives. Think how much money they could have socked away in IRAs and bonds and never really missed it. But when her husband died, she had nothing because they had spent every last penny they had.

# You Gotta Take Care

Psalm 15:1~ God, who can dwell in your tent? Who can live on your holy mountain?

15:2 ~ The one who walks with integrity, who acts according to what is right,

15: 3 ~ who speaks truth from her heart, and does not let slander tread on her tongue,

15:4 ~ who has not acted wrongly to any creature, does not cast reproach upon any kin,

15:5 ~ for whom that which God rejects, is like stolen plunder in her eyes,

15: 6 ~ the one who reveres all who hold the Eternal in awe,

15:7 ~ who takes an oath about another's wrongdoing without retracting out of fear,

15:8 ~ who does not lend silver at interest, and a bribe against the innocent will not accept.

15: 9 ~ The one who does this will never stumble as long as she lives.[7]

So many black sisters and brothers are living on wages next to slave labor, that the idea of saving any of their money is no more than an idea. They barely have enough to live on. Some of us manage to work your way out of the poverty trap, or our children do, but too many of you still don't know how to save. If you have spent your life living from hand to mouth, when money does begin to come in you don't know any other way to live, except from hand to mouth. If you have been trying to keep body and on wages that wouldn't keep a bird alive, when you do manage to find a job or start a business that pays, you have to watch it. It is far to easy to spend and spend, because you have been living on deficit for too long, and you

7    Pamela Greenberg; The Complete Book of Psalms; Bloomsbury USA, New York; 2010

want to fill that empty place inside you. You are so afraid of being poor, of having to do without those things that you need, that you surround yourselves with stuff. Enough stuff that it would take two or three lifetimes to use it all. But we can only count on having this one lifetime.

Some people cannot walk through a store without hearing every item on the shelves and racks calling to them, "Take me home—take me home!" They buy shoes to go with dresses that they might be able to wear after they have lost twenty to thirty pounds. They buy hats they will never wear and scarves and shirts that get piled into closets and chests and forgotten, because those things are so deeply buried under so much other stuff that they don't even know what they have any more. Sometimes, especially if they were deprived as children, they derive a sense of security from having all their stuff piled high and deep around them when they walk into their apartments.

I learned some things about what it means to save when I worked for that Jewish couple. Oh yes, they had money to spend. But they invested a lot of their money in things I hadn't even heard of. When they were young they wanted to make sure that no matter what happened, they would have some money to live on. So by the time I met them, they were these two wonderful elderly people who knew they had enough money saved and invested that they could choose how they would be taken care of when they were at last too old to be able to take care of themselves. Now, that is real independence.

That was why, when Brandon and I got together, we decided to save some of our money every week. I made more money than he did, so I saved two hundred dollars every week and he saved one hundred dollars. And that made a total of three hundred dollars we put into savings, every single week. We budgeted the rest of our money. We used to spend twenty-five dollars every month on our meat and seventy-five dollars a month on the rest of our groceries. And we didn't buy any junk food.

My mother, who I have always loved but who I could not always understand, and my aunt Rose worked to look good. For them this was most important, and they were both elegant women. I could understand why my mother and my aunt believed it was important for a woman to be expensively groomed and elegantly dressed, and I learned a lot about such things, just living around them. But I believed it was more important to be frugal.

The first apartment Brandon and I had was in an elderly woman's home. That was the year my mom and dad decided they were going to move to Georgia. They begged me to come down there with them. Aunt Rose was going with them and they were taking my old bedroom furniture, as they wanted to make it clear to me that there would always be a place for me in their home if I ever needed to live with them. But, I felt more than ready to stand on my own, and even though Brandon and I were not married yet, we felt pretty secure together.

The old lady whose basement we were renting might have been messing with Voodoo, or she might have just been crazy. I call people like her cranks, which doesn't really say much about them. Still, I don't like to speak evil of people, especially when it is not necessary. This landlady gave us a picture to brighten up our basement apartment. It was pretty. There were a lot of pink flowers in it. I hung it up over our bed and didn't think anything more of it. But almost from the very first night that picture hung over our bed, Brandon started having horrible nightmares. He said there were demons and snakes chasing him in his dreams. He'd wake up every night screaming, sweating and shaking. I had never seen him like that before and he said he had never been like that before. We were both bewildered, so we prayed. I was on my way to work one morning when God told me to go back home and take that picture down. I took the picture down and buried it in back of a closet. Brandon had no more nightmares after that.

It isn't easy to figure out what God wants of you when the world is such a crazy place. The woman who owned that basement apartment made life interesting for us in a number of ways. Brandon and I were beginning to collect some nice things, though the neighborhood was rougher than it looked, with a crack-house on nearly every corner. We were paying that lady a fair sum of money for that little apartment and we wanted to know that our things would be safe when we went to work. There was no door to separate our apartment from hers. So, we had a door put in, with a good lock. She was upset that we had put the door up, but we believed we had done her a favor by putting it in. As long as she was renting that space as an apartment she would have to insure that her tenants had some privacy. She was the landlady, so we had to give her a key for it. After all, it was her house. But I was never happy about that, because she would come into our apartment while we were at work and snoop around. It wasn't long before Brandon and I decided it was time to move on.

I wanted to move into a co-op in Rochdale. We needed about eight or nine thousand dollars to do this, and we had to fill out an application and let them check our credit. I talked with one of my cousins about this and she said she would help us out. She was old enough to be my mother. In fact she had a daughter who was about two years older than me. We shared a two bedroom apartment with her. I had a phone installed in the room Brandon and I shared. I kept that phone locked in our bedroom, but I needed it to be able to stay in contact with the people I worked for. She found it and told me I would either have to get rid of that phone or move out of her home. For reasons I could never figure out; ignorance? she had decided I was using that phone to spy on her. We had so many arguments about crazy stuff. It was as though her brain had been screwed in backwards.

One thing I have seen again and again is that all you sisters carry around such deep anger. We've seen things that would make a saint want to kill. Mostly we are in no position to be able to fight the real causes of our problems, which are created by a mix of many things; from old-fashioned fear and prejudice to corporations taking jobs away from everyone, and a legal system that appears to have only one purpose—to keep good black men behind bars for most of their lives. How do you fight all that? It's too big to fight by ourselves, so instead we fight each other. We do crazy-stupid things to each other, just to keep us down. In the King James Bible, Romans 1:28 & 29 says, And even as they did not like to retain God in their knowledge, God gave them over to a reprobate mind to do those things which are not convenient (fitting). Being filled with all unrighteousness, fornication, wickedness, covetousness; full of envy, deceit and gossip.

That is quite a list of negative stuff! Just keep God in your heart. In whatever way you know. Keep that spirit in your heart and it will be easier to keep your heart open to the love around you.

Everyone I know has a relative or a friend like that—someone who is paranoid and delusional. It's no wonder black kids grow up feeling so mixed and confused. Part of it is from not really knowing who they are and part of it is from living with adults who are not only ignorant but delusional.

I wanted to have children. Sometimes I would look at this man who had vowed to be with me through sickness and health and a cold chill would go down my back over the thought that I would be spending the rest of my life with him. For better or worse, he and I would be eternally bound, even if we chose to get divorced, we would be bound to each other by the experiences we shared. No one could break those bonds.

My life was not complete. That age old desire to be fruitful and multiply reared its head—I wanted a baby. More than anything else, I wanted a baby. Looking at Brandon it was easy to see that he would be a good daddy. We wouldn't be a complete family until we had a child. I had already had a few abortions, and those experiences made my desire to have a child of our own all the more.

I did all I could to let it happen. And then I got pregnant. I had a little boy. Giving birth was painful like the abortions had been, but far different and extremely profound. It was as though the world had been split in two and there was all my life before our baby was born, and all my life to come after the baby.

Brandon and I brought him home from the hospital and for a few blessed weeks we felt as though our little family was complete. He was a tiny scrap of angel. I fed him and changed him and watched him begin to grow. I got up in the middle of the night and walked the floor with him when his piercing cries would have wakened the dead. And then one morning I went in to check on him, as it seemed he had been sleeping for too long. I picked him up and found his limbs were stiff, and when I shook and patted him, it was obvious his soul had fled.

SIDS the doctors said. Sudden Infant Death Syndrom. No one understands much about it. Some people believe the baby becomes severely depressed and no longer wants to live. What would you have to do to a baby to make it want to leave life before he'd even had a chance to taste it? Sometimes I've wondered whether the three abortions I'd had only a few years earlier had caused changes to occur in my body's chemistry that would not permit me to bear a child who could live. In fact, I lost not one baby but two to SIDS, and I've often thought God must have wanted me to learn something from that experience, or I would not have had to go through it twice over. At least one of the lessons I learned was that every life is precious. We're all God's children and we've got to begin to not only treat each other as though this is true, but ourselves. Even so, I about gave up on having children and concentrated on work and building a business.

I was lucky to have an uncle who was a good man. He owned a roofing company and he told me about a school bus I could buy. He said, "Don't be afraid of what people think. Just buy it and get yourself in business." And that bus was the beginning of the business I own and run today.

That's the thing—you can't be worrying about what people think when they're crazy. You just do what you know is right for you. My cousin and I had so many arguments that couldn't be sorted out because her mind was messed up. I don't know what cocktail of drugs she had been feeding it all her life, or how paranoid she was—but there are some people you just cannot reason with. Their brains have gone out to lunch and their heads are empty, waiting to fill up with evil stuff. I feel badly for such people and anyone who has to live with them. They make life miserable for everyone around them.

Brandon's mother can be like that. When I first got together with her son, back when I was working at the hospital and he had just got out of the Phoenix House, we went to TJ Max and I bought a bunch of blue jeans and shirts—things that matched so we could dress alike sometimes. I spent a few hundred dollars on clothes for him, cause he needed them. Then we went back to his mother's home. She was so angry with me for buying clothes for her son. She yelled at me, saying I should have bought insurance for his car instead. When I told my daddy about that he was dumfounded. "That car is not yours and you don't drive it. What does she mean you should buy insurance for it?"

That car has a sad story behind it. Brandon had saved a good bit of money when he was working, before he was sent off to Phoenix House. He was a sixteen-year-old kid and he had been living at home, so he didn't have much of anything else to do with his money. He put it in the bank, and when he came home from Phoenix House, the money was gone. His mother told him, "The money is gone, but here's the car. It's yours." His mother had got her hands on his money and spent it, then she bought him the car for a couple hundred dollars as a consolation prize.

I do try to be nice to that woman. Sometimes I think she would even make Jesus weep over the things she does. I remember my mother telling me, sometime before she died, that I should feed that lady with a long-handled spoon. Visions of ten foot poles come to mind—as in, I wouldn't touch her with one. But I think my mother meant that I should be nice to the woman, but keep my distance. I guess that boils down to being good to myself so that I have the energy and the resources to be good to others.

I look back on those years and see there are lots of things I could have done better. But one thing I have always liked to do is pay my bills. I cannot trust that my man will always be with me, or that he will always be able to work and take care of me. So, I do what I can to make sure I have an income and can pay my own bills. I chose to be like the virtuous woman described in Proverbs 31:10-31. Lots of Christian men would like their wives to stay at home and let their men take care of everything that is not housework and childcare. They forget that the good wife knows how to work at many things.

31:13 She seeks wool and flax and works with willing hands. 31:14 She is like the ships of the merchant and brings her food from afar. 31:16 She considers a field and buys it. With the fruit of her hands she plants a vineyard. 31:17 She dresses herself with strength and makes her arms strong. 31:18 She perceives that her merchandise is profitable. Her lamp does not go out at night.

I believe verse 18 may be the most important of these verses for most of us today. We need to know how to get along in the business world in order to survive. This verse presents an idea that many women have a very hard time learning. Her merchandise is profitable. Those things that she is able to do well are worth doing because they can be profitable. Those things that she most wants to learn how to do are worth her learning, because they can be profitable. The other verses are wonderful, speaking of being generous with your family and your neighbors and acting honorably, as your entire family will benefit by that. Most important, the excellent wife described in these verses values herself and what she can do.

We all know what the golden rule is. Do unto others as you would have others do unto you. However, women have been taught all their lives that others—other people—are more important than they are. It's partly why I was so willing and eager to throw myself away on Keith when I was a young girl, no matter what kind of pain that created for me and my family. As women, we are all too ready to undervalue ourselves. A wise woman once said that for women the Golden Rule should be turned around to say, Do unto yourself as you would do unto others. If you would be generous with your next door neighbor, lending her food or money, make sure you have food and money for yourself. When bad things happen to a friend and you let her cry on your shoulder and you pray with her, don't be afraid to let yourself cry when harsh things happen. Give yourself a chance to heal and pray. It's about learning to be as gentle and caring with yourself as you would wish other people to be with you. It's because you cannot truly love anyone else—even God—until you know how to love yourself. It is also about keeping yourself ready to do God's bidding. Remember the parable of the ten virgins. Each of them had a lamp they must keep lit and filled with oil through the night, so that they could meet their bridegroom. You are the lamp you must keep filled and ready for God when he calls upon you to act. You cannot let yourself be gone on drugs, or broken down with shame, guilt and depression. The counselors at Phoenix House helped me to understand this, and the more Brandon and I worked to build our lives, the better we understood it. These lines are Matthew 25:1-13

1. Then shall the kingdom of heaven be likened unto ten virgins, who took their lamps, and went forth to meet the bridegroom.
2. And five of them were foolish, and five were wise.
3. For the foolish, when they took their lamps, took no oil with them:
4. But the wise took oil in their vessels with their lamps.
5. Now while the bridegroom tarried, they all slumbered and slept.
6. But at midnight there is a cry, Behold, the bridegroom! Come ye forth to meet him.
7. Then all those virgins arose, and trimmed their lamps.
8. And the foolish said unto the wise, Give us of your oil; for our lamps are going out.
9. But the wise answered, saying, Peradventure there will not be enough for us and you: go ye rather to them that sell, and buy for yourselves.
10. And while they went away to buy, the bridegroom came; and they that were ready went in with him to the marriage feast: and the door was shut.
11. Afterward came also the other virgins, saying, Lord, Lord, open to us.
12. But he answered and said, Verily I say unto you, I know you not.
13. Watch therefore, for ye know not the day nor the hour.[8]

---

[8] American Standard Version

An apartment did become available at a decent price, but it was too close to where my cousin lived, and I really wanted to get away from that. Brandon and I did find an apartment around the corner and my Uncle Al put a new ceiling up and installed a fan in our living room. He did excellent work and even the landlord liked it.

Brandon had been doing odd jobs for a while, working at whatever he could get that would help pay our bills. Some Haitians he worked with told him about a job he could have making deliveries for Budweiser.

I was still working for that nice Jewish couple when I got pregnant with my son. After I had lost two beautiful babies within days after bringing them home from the hospital, I did not know whether to thank the good Lord, or to worry, over the fact that I was pregnant again. Many years ago, when women took for granted that they would be likely to lose half the children they gave birth to, before those children reached the age of five, many families did not name their children until long after they were born. They wanted to be sure those children would live, before they gave them a name and permitted them to have a personality.

The gentleman I was taking care of knew I was pregnant before I was ready to admit that I was. He was very pleased. He and his wife went out of their way so that I would not have to do anything that might hurt the baby I was carrying. They knew how precious that child was to me, even if I did have some misgivings. One afternoon, he placed his hands on my belly and said a blessing over it—Baruch atah adonai . . . I don't remember all the words he said, but those first three words are Hebrew for Blessings flow through you, Lord. Then he gave that big, wide grin of his and said, "Now you have a Jewish baby."

We named our son for his father; Brandon, and watched him every day, when we brought him home from the hospital. I could not bear it if another child of mine died in infancy. Something about that old man's blessing took, for our son grew strong and healthy. He was also highly intelligent and studious, just as you would expect a good Jewish boy to be.

Seven years later, in 2003, my mother-in-law's house burned down. I was pregnant with my little girl at the time. My mother-in-law had no place to go, so she came to stay with us for a while. I let her use my bedroom, and that would have been all right, if she had only been there for three or four days. But you know that even for the best of us, it can take a few months to find a place to live. My mother-in-law can be a difficult woman anyway. The longer she was there the more uncomfortable it got for me. I was sleeping on the couch while my pregnant belly grew bigger and more demanding. Each night it was harder to put up with sleeping on that couch than it had been the night before. And our mother-in-law slept in our bedroom on our great big bed as though she belonged there. Then during the day she would complain about the way I kept my apartment, complaining about my keeping too much food in the freezer and the fact that I kept the place too clean to suit her. She is the living example of one who sows bitterness, and is only beginning to learn that—Be not deceived; God is not mocked: for whatsoever a man soweth, that shall he also reap.[9]

I was twenty-seven years old when I got married. My mother and father made it into a celebration to beat all celebrations. Relatives came round to visit that I

---

9    Galatians 6:7; American Standard Version.

hadn't even heard of. My mother got together with Brandon's mother and had a good time in the kitchen with her, cooking and washing dishes. That was when she told me that I would have to feed that woman with a long handled spoon. I was never certain what my mother meant by that, and I never had a chance to ask her before she died. I suspect she meant that I should be nice to my mother-in-law, but that I should keep my distance because that woman bites. And truly, I have seen her in action. A spoon with a handle at least ten feet long would be ideal. So, I be nice to her and keep my distance.

Brandon and I are both nice shades of cocoa brown. I'd say we are about the same color—he and I. We're also about the same color his mother is, though she may be a little darker now that she's getting older. But she's complained that I'm too dark for her family and she's disappointed that Brandon didn't marry someone who was lighter. Anyone who doesn't know how Black people think would say that she was being pretty silly. The thing is, she comes out of a time when the more easily a body could pass for white, the better he would be able to survive. Black men, no matter how well qualified they are to do something, don't get hired as easily as white men who have the same qualifications. They don't get hired and they don't generally get paid the way white men do.

In one of the old TV reality shows, the executives hired some expert make-up artists to make a white family—mother, father and children—look black and a black family look white. Then they turned the two families loose to live in a neighborhood where nobody knew them. Each family essentially traded races with the other. The white family came out of that experience saying they had never understood what it meant to have to deal with prejudice until then. The black man came out of it almost weeping. He said that for the first time in his life he could walk into a store or an employment office and be treated like a human being.

So, while some of us don't want anything to do with light skinned blacks, there are others who insist that their children marry as light as possible. The truth is, God doesn't look at the color of our skin, or whether our hair is straight or nappy. He looks at what's in our hearts. God is spirit and He has no color. You could say He is the color of water.

For all I complain about her, my mother-in-law isn't all bad. Her birthday came around soon after Brandon and I were married. I tried to figure out what to give her for a gift. I thought of a number of things and finally gave her a copy of the Bible. Now, when she sees Brandon, she'll point to that book and say, "You should read this too."

That woman came from a hard family. When her mother, Brandon's grandmother, died of Black Lung disease from breathing in too much coal dust where she worked. The insurance company gave them a settlement of several thousand dollars. Her sister and brother proceeded to cheat her out of her share of that money. Whether those guys learned to cheat like that from their parents, I don't know. In Proverbs, it says that the sins of the fathers will be visited onto the children unto the seventh generation. People down through the ages have asked why God would pass sins down through a family like that. But when you think about it you realize that when parents teach their children bad things and neglect or abuse them, those children are likely to grow up and do the same thing again to their children. So, sins do get passed down from one generation to the next.

# Putting it All Together

---❖❖---

1 Samuel 12:20 ~ And Samuel said unto the people, Fear not: ye have done all this wickedness: yet turn not aside from following the LORD, but serve the LORD with all your heart.

Both my marriage and my business were doing well. I owned a Mercedes Benz bus, while Davon and Thomas, who could have done so much with their lives, had nothing. Thomas tried to get back at the world for having kept him in prison for so long by getting together with a girl. He promised her everything and then took her income tax money to buy himself a Mercedes Benz truck.

When I was little, I felt so secure that my brothers were there taking care of me. Now that they were home from prison, it was as though the proverbial seven devils had infested their souls. I gave them clothes and a place to stay. I gave them thousand dollar checks so they could get some of the things they needed. But their rage came out over anything and nothing. I had not been in prison for the years and years that they had been, and I was again lucky when I got out, that I was sent to Phoenix House where my anger could defuse, before I tried to enter society again.

We expect prisoners to be able to act and be normal (whatever normal is) when they get out. It isn't possible. They just got through spending years of their lives, at best just marking time in an eight by ten cell. At worst, they were fighting for their lives. The best a lot of these guys can do is pray to the Good Lord for guidance.

Guys who come out of war zones suffer from what we call PTSD, or Post Traumatic Stress Disorder, and I would bet the things my brothers had to deal with in prison left them with that same problem. However, they weren't willing to talk, and I didn't know how to listen at that time. Perhaps if they could have had treatment for that problem soon after they were released, they could have pulled themselves together sooner. Thomas and Davon are still having problems dealing with the real world. It is as though they have lost their compassion and they just want to take and take, as though surrounding themselves with stuff could rid them of their nightmares.

Davon and Thomas were both so full of hate when they came out of prison, I hardly recognized them. They weren't the men they had been when they were sent up. Thomas, from being the man who refused to lay the blame on his cousin for transporting the gun and the cocaine, was consumed with jealousy when he got out. As far as he could see, the entire world had moved on while he marked time in an eight by ten cell, sitting there among guys whose dreams and hopes and desire to create and build had been punched and beaten down by the other inmates of that institution and by the guards who all demonstrated a sadistic streak, no matter how humane they may have been before they went to work for the system.

My mother took my brothers in for a while. She had the space, and she had some money. But it surely wasn't easy. After all those years of prison, they were angry at the whole world. Prison had been great for teaching them how to hurt other people and not to care about it. Their wounds are only beginning to heal. Some of those wounds run so deep only God can touch them. But Davon now has a photography business that he really likes, and that is good. It is more than good—it's a miracle.

In the United States, more than six out of every ten black men go to prison. Black women are not too far behind, in terms of prison experience. The United States imprisons more of its population than any other country in the world. This is the only country in the world where prison is a way of life for its black and brown people. It means that we have to work a whole lot harder to stay out of prison than most other people. And, we have to learn how to help each other stay out of prison. We need to understand that God wants us to be really good to each other, because if we don't, the law isn't going to help us and the government isn't going to help us. We need to learn to help ourselves and help each other.

Some of us have a heavy load of things we'd like to forget. Prison is a shit-load of stuff to forget. Any situation that permits abuse with no let-up kills spirit.

Parents leave us with their baggage. They really don't mean to do it. We carry all the mistakes they made. The things they told us when we were growing up, such as; "You're stupid," or, You're no good," come back to haunt us every time life knocks us down. We need to fill our heads and hearts with good things, such as; "We are good, strong, capable people." Goodness knows, we have to be strong in order to be able to put up with the shit that life dishes out. I don't know anyone who does not believe, on some level, that he or she will live forever. After all, being alive is all we know about. Preparing for your death? That's like not living any more.

My mother lived a rich and full life. She loved all her family and did everything she could to help her sisters and her children. We can't blame her for dying and leaving her will seemingly so messed up, the way she did. Death comes to all of us, and some of us are better prepared than others. She traveled all over the world. When she was forty-five, she met and married a twenty-five-year-old Jamaican fellow. They must have loved each other at least long enough to say I do in front of a Justice of the Peace. Now, we have to fight this fellow for her pension money.

Down through the years she bought an assortment of jewelry and a mink coat. The coat was a beautiful keepsake of my mother's and at least some of the jewelry was very expensive. She had always told me that these things would one day belong to me and my little girl. But, a couple years before she died, she gave it to my Aunt R___ to use. I never insisted that this aunt give it back to me while my mother was alive. We all understood that she would return it to me when my mother died.

A few days after the funeral, I asked this aunt for the jewelry. She looked at me and said, "It's safe with me!"

I told her, "By midnight, you give it either to the preacher or his wife. Just make sure I get the stuff.

Aunt R___ came over a few hours later to give the jewelry and the coat to my dad. Yeah—maybe I could have been nicer about that stuff, but I had to learn how to fight and defend what I believed was right, from the day my two older brothers were first sent to prison. And those months I spent in prison didn't teach me a thing about manners or what people call diplomacy. I come across flat-footed, and tell it the way I see it. Aunt R___. Has not spoken to me since.

But, I'm really upset with her for not speaking to my father any more. He and my mother helped her when she didn't have any other place to go. I have even written checks to this aunt for several hundred dollars when she had no other way to get money for her bills, and she was always grateful for it.

I figure that when I love someone, I love them whether they are up or down. That is the way it is, or it isn't love. But this aunt of mine hasn't spoken to either my dad or me since. He wasn't the one who insisted about Mother's things; it was me. I don't understand how she could just write off an old man like my father, and not have anything more to do with him, when he took her in and made sure she had a decent place to stay and good food to eat, until she was ready to stand on her own feet.

Speaking of my mother's death makes me think of the legacies we leave our children. Most of us don't know who we are or where we came from. Too often, we don't know who our grandparents are. A lot of us don't even know who our grandparents were, because our parents don't know, or if they do, they are too ashamed to tell us. There's a good bit of that shame in my family. I love my mother dearly, and I have always understood her to be a proud and capable woman, full of wisdom. Certainly she was a woman who would sacrifice her own happiness and comfort for her sisters and brothers and her children.

She never did marry the man who is my father, even though they lived and worked together for many years. My brothers and I grew up never using my father's sir-name. Our last name was the one that belonged to my mother's first husband. But her first husband wasn't our father.

I don't know what my father thought of these goings on, but he was a good and faithful husband to her and the only father I have ever known. He had his principles though, and he had a temper to defend them with. He may not have been the easiest man for a woman to live with, but he cherished all his children.

I wrote some about the young man in Jamaica whom she married. She would go off to visit him whenever things got to be too rough and uncomfortable in New York City for her. I remember that she made a lot of trips back to Jamaica. She used to travel all over the world and everywhere she went she would watch to see how people cooked so she could bring back fabulous recipes to use for the fine dinners she held at her supper club.

My father always had a surly attitude towards fancy food, more than likely because she picked up a lot of her recipes when she went off to Jamaica. Meat and potatoes, maybe some good fried chicken—those things were enough to satisfy a man's hunger as far as he was concerned. My mother brought back some seasoning sticks from one of her Jamaican trips, which you couldn't buy in a grocery store around here. On her return she made a meal that was so good it made you want to slap someone, or weep. But all my father said was, "I don't want no sticks in my food."

I don't know whether he knew about my mother's boy-toy in Jamaica. If he did he never let on. But he must have suspected. On the other hand, my mother robbed us when she refused to let our real daddy's name go on our birth certificates, as there was a legacy connected with my real father that my brothers and I have been fighting to get for a number of years.

The truly sad thing is that when people tell you all your life that you're stupid and can't do much and can't learn much, you tend to live down to those expectations. And, you forget just how creative and intelligent you really are.

Let's go back just a little bit in history. In order to survive slavery and be here today to tell about it, we had to be intelligent. We had to be strong and we had to be resourceful and resilient. We had to know when to fight, and we had to know when to lay low. And every time we fell down or were ground down, we had to be ready to pick ourselves up off the floor again. All of that takes uncommon strength. But then, weren't we made in God's image?

We've been hurt so many times that we begin to feel that being hurt is normal. We begin to believe that it is not right that any of our Black sisters and brothers should do well in life—especially when they wind up having more that we have. So then, some of us lash out in anger and try to tear them down. When we learn how to stand up for each other and help each other, we will begin to heal from all the wounds.

Right after the Civil War, back when the Emancipation Proclamation really did mean something, there were Black people busily teaching themselves how to read and how to speak and write good, clean English. Black people were teaching themselves how to be engineers. And there were Black politicians and Black legislatures across the South. I know, it sounds almost impossible, because it didn't last long. The elite in White society got scared. They didn't want anyone toppling them down from their pinnacles. They got together in towns and cities across the South and formed the Klu Klux Klan, in order to keep poor people, and specifically black people, groveling on their hands and knees.

Well, before the worst of the backlash came down, my great, great granddaddy bought some land in Alabama, right where Tuskagee Institute now stands. It was four hundred acres that had been a plantation before the war, off in the hinterlands. Nobody thought that land was worth much, or he wouldn't have been able to buy it.

You have to remember that only a few years before he bought that land, he'd been living as a slave. You see, my great, great granddaddy had a vision. Even though he'd lived most of his life as someone else's property, he believed in the power of Black people to succeed. Together with Booker T. Washington he helped to establish what we know as Tuskagee Institute. Now, my real daddy is a direct descendent of that man.

All our ancestors were good, brave people—and tough. They had to be tough in order to survive. They were smart. Some of them taught themselves how to read and write better than a lot of people coming out of expensive universities can now. But freedom doesn't come for free. We have to work for it and we have to teach out children to work for it.

# Truth Telling

———◈✦◈———

Psalm 15:1 ~ Lord, who shall abide in thy tabernacle? who shall dwell in thy holy hill?

2 ~ He that walketh uprightly, and worketh righteousness, and speaketh the truth in his heart.

3 ~ He that backbiteth not with his tongue, nor doeth evil to his neighbor, nor taketh up a reproach against his neighbor.

4 ~ In whose eyes a vile person is contemned ; but he honoureth them that fear the Lord. He that sweareth to his own hurt, and changeth not.

5 ~ He that putteth not out his money to usury, nor taketh reward against the innocent. He that doeth these things shall never be moved.

I am writing this book from a Christian perspective, because it is through Jesus that I have found the grace to pull my life together in ways that help not only me and my family, but the people around me and the people I teach. I suppose I could have found grace through any number of religions, but none of those other religions spoke to me the way the gospel of Jesus speaks to me.

I want everyone who reads this book to set their minds on thinking big, because, through God and Jesus, all things are possible. Without the spiritual connection we haven't got much. Even when you have lots of money, and you can go out and buy all the pretty things you might ever want, none of that will make you happy without the spiritual connection. Gandhi once said that our politics are a reflection of our religion. I say that everything we do in our lives is a reflection of our religion.

My Aunt Alma had a stroke and lived on for twenty-two years, paralyzed from her neck down. Uncle Al took good care of her till the day he died. He made sure she could stay at home with round-the-clock nursing care, and that she was always comfortable. However, she could no longer be his wife in the usual way, and Uncle Al wanted to share his life with a woman who could share with him. He took up with Eva, a woman who had been friends with both of them for years before Alma had her stroke. He and Eva had children together and he took care of all of them as though they were his family. I will not deny that taking care of two women gave my uncle a difficult row-to-hoe. Through all those years he continued to take care of Alma. He had, after all, made the promise to take care of her in sickness and in health. But, he started another family. It was with a woman and children who I am certain he loved and who loved him in return. Eva was not a one night stand in any sense of the word.

When Uncle Al died, my mother asked me to write the obituary. Alma was still alive. She had taken care of me many times when I was a little girl and had been one of those people I could look up to and talk things over with when my mother couldn't be there. My mother wanted me to mention Eva along with Alma in the obituary. I sat down and tried to write it, but every time I got to the part about being survived by his wife and children, I couldn't bring myself to talk about his mistress and the children he had with her. I prayed about it and realized that if I did talk about Eva and her children it would make trouble between them and the children he'd had with Alma.

My mother loves her family. She would do everything for them. She told me, "You know Al would have wanted Eva in the obituary."

I stood my ground. "Al's dead. I'm not going to put a curse on my life. If I talk about Eva in there, I would cause problems for all of Al's children. I'm not going to do that."

Some people might not agree with the decision I made then. But I had to follow my conscience. You see, there is a spiritual way to deal with your family. There is a spiritual way to deal with the community around you, and there is a spiritual way to deal with money. It is about how we relate to God. Everything I do is spiritual. It is up to each of us to listen to what the Lord tells us, and to follow that in the best way we can.

Not long ago, my daughter's teacher called me in for a conference. My husband and I drove down to the school, wondering whether our little girl was in trouble. She is a bright, energetic six-year-old child, whom God has blessed with a wonderful intelligence and creativity, and whose heart and soul are big enough and wide enough that she loves everyone she meets. Her teacher doesn't know what to do about this. You see, Brittany does not fit her stereotype as to what a black child should be like. No matter how hard that woman works to fit my little girl into her cramped little box of pre-conceived notions, that child just pops out again. My husband thought he would have to entertain the teacher, and he was all set to talk for hours. I told him, "No. God tells me there isn't anything wrong. In fact, we're going to this conference for nothing."

Her teacher opened the conference by telling us that she was very concerned over our Brittany. For one thing, the child went around acting as though she didn't have a care in the world.

This did cause me to sit up a bit. "Well, isn't that the way a six-year-old child is supposed to act?"

Her teacher gave us a highly supercilious look and went on to say that Brittany had been talking in school about the nice apartment we have in New York City. She added that we need to teach our child not to make up stories, because everyone knows black people don't live that way.

At this point she was staring down her nose so hard that her eyes were crossed. Words like prejudice and black empowerment began to dance through my head. "The truth is, Miss ___, we do have a nice apartment in New York City. We have that apartment because my husband and I choose to live as God shows us. We act as He teaches and works through us. Brittany has not been making up stories."

Her teacher did quiet down somewhat, and that supercilious look on her face began to fade. She was almost a nice looking woman when her eyes uncrossed. I asked her, "How many black children have you taught?"

"Your Brittany is the first one."

"Well, let me give you some advice. Don't try to put them into your stereotype about black children, and maybe they won't put you into their stereotype about white teachers."

You see, nobody wants to be held responsible for their mistakes. But the only way to fix something that is wrong, is to first of all look at the mistakes you made, and then own what you need to do to make things right. That means taking charge of what you are going to do. It is easier to do this, when you know you are following the path the Lord has set for you. I accepted Jesus in my heart when I was eight-years-old. Jesus might or might not be the way you want to think about what's eternal and true. It has been said that when the Jews left Egypt, after their four hundred years of slavery, they stood on the brink of the shore of the Red Sea, not knowing what to do next. One of the old men headed out into the water till it was up to his knees, and his wife called out to him, "Keep going!" So, he continued into the water, until it was up to his hips, and his wife called out to him, "Keep going!" He shrugged his shoulders, turned around, and continued walking till the water was up to his chest. He looked back to shore again, and his wife called out to him, "Keep going!" So, he continued walking across until the water was up to his chin. What did his wife say when he looked back to shore? "Keep going!" It was then that Moses raised his hand and God separated the waters. Some say that there was more than one path through those waters. In other words, there is more than one way to meet God. The important thing is to build a good, strong relationship with Him. For that is what will keep you going when times get rough.

# *Biblical Finances*

John: 2:13-16

13—And the Jews' passover was at hand, and Jesus went up to Jerusalem,

14—And found in the temple those that sold oxen and sheep and doves, and the changers of money sitting—

15—And when he had made a scourge of small chords, he drove them all out of the temple, and the sheep and the oxen, and poured out the changers of money, and overthrew the tables;

16—And said unto them that sold doves, Take these things hence; make not my father's house a house of merchants. [10]

Proverbs 3:9

Honor the Lord with thy substance (wealth), and with the first fruits of all thine increase.

Matthew 25:14-29

14—For it will be like a man going on a journey, who called his servants and entrusted them his property.

15—To one he gave five talents, to another two, to another one; to each according to his ability. Then he went away.

16—He who had received the five talents went at once and traded with them, and he made five talents more.

17—So also, he who had the two talents made two talents more.

---

[10]   KJV

18—But he who had received the one talent went and dug in the ground and hid his master's money.

19—Now after a long time, the master came and settled accounts with them.

20—And he who had received the five talents came forward, bringing five talents more, saying, 'Master, you have delivered me five talents. Here, I have made five talents more.'

21—His master said to him, 'Well done, good and faithful servant. You have been faithful over little, I will set you over much. Enter into the joy of your master.'

22—And he also who had two talents came to his master, saying, 'Master, you delivered two talents; here I have made two talents more.'

23—His master said to him, 'Well done, good and faithful servant. You have been faithful over a little, I will set you over much. Enter into the joy of your master.'

24—He also who had received the one talent came forward, saying, 'Master, I knew you to be a hard man, reaping where you did not sow, and gathering where you did not scatter seed.

25—so I was afraid, and I went and hid your talent in the ground. Here you have what is yours.'

26—But his master said, 'You wicked and slothful servant! You knew that I reap where I have not sown and gather where I have scattered no seed?

27—Then you ought to have invested my money with the bankers, and at my coming I should have received what was my own with interest.

28—So, take the talent from him and give it to him who has the ten talents.

29—For to everyone who has will more be given, and he will have an abundance. But from the one who has not, even what he has will be taken away.[11]

---

[11]   ESV

The getting and spending of money can be harsh. It generally feels as though we get less than we need These parables that Jesus tells concerning money can leave one feeling a little cold, depending on what their feelings are concerning money as a means of trade. Granted, most preachers like to say that this parable does not refer to money at all, but to those God-gicen abilities that you were born with. Some people have a marvelous talent for music. Other people have talents for painting, or writing or building, or a talent to help people feel good with themselves. If you do not develop those talents, you never get the benefit of them, nor can you use them to help anyone else.

I put this parable under money, because that is the way life works. Our government taxes those who have little money far more than it taxes those who have a lot. Stores located in poor neighborhoods often charge two and three times as much as the stores in wealthy neighborhoods. Banks charge the small accounts much more heavily than they charge the large accounts, for the same services. It is not right, it is simply the way it is.

A talent was a unit of money equivalent to about twenty years of common labor. In today's currency, that one talent would be about four to six hundred thousand dollars. That would certainly be enough cash to do some interesting things. Earlier, I quoted a passage from Proverbs about the good woman. The woman who knows how to work with her hands and to buy and sell in the marketplace to earn what she needs so that she can take care of her family and her household. Such a woman is said to be more precious than jewels. This woman puts time and attention into developing her talents—those things she loves to do, for they will nourish her life and the lives of her children far more than expensive toys will.

Until God transformed my life, I didn't know what it means to live a rich life. Sure, when I was a kid, I had all the clothes and food and things that I needed, but in the ways that count, my life was not rich at all.

We have all heard the saying, Money is the root of all evil. I beg to differ—Greed is the root of all evil. Without money, we cannot pay our rent or buy our food or take our kids to the doctor when they get sick. Some people talk about the money junkies on Wall street who have to have their money fix, just the way some people I know have to have their drug fix. And like junkies everywhere, those Wall Street junkies don't care who they hurt, or how many people they hurt, as long as they get their fix. My father used to say, Money needs a boss. Someone has to be in charge of how we use it and what we do to get it. the best someone for that is God.

Money is an agreed upon unit of trade. I believe that if we all understood where money comes from—that greedy bankers manufacture it by lending it at interest, so that they can have more, even when there really isn't any more. If we knew that those bankers do not care at all what happens to the rest of us, we would choose not to use their money at all. For most of us, that would not be possible. We have to use it. We have no choice, if we are going to pay the rent, buy a car, keep our families fed and send our children to school, we have to use money. Money comes to us already tainted with greed from the bankers who control it. I make sure that the money I earn I earn honestly. I will not swindle anyone and I will not cheat my clients. As a bus driver, my job was to get children safely to and from school, and that is what I did.

But, maybe that isn't what your job is supposed to be. What you do to earn the money you need to live is up to you and God. The best way to find out what God has in mind for your life is to pray, and keep your inner ears open to what He tells you. The thing is, you want to be alert to what is happening, and to remember— you are God's hands and feet. When you know God wants you to do something, it's up to you to get up and do it in the best way you can.

God is not a giant vending machine in the sky, waiting for us to put our nickels in, so that He can give us that Mercedes Benz that is taking up so much space up there in the clouds. Prayer is meant to keep our minds and hearts open so that we can find ways to do and be that are better than we have been doing. No matter how well we are living our lives, we can always improve. Prayer—talking to God and listening for that still, small voice—can show us ways we can build better relationships with our families, be good friends to our neighbors and work we can do that is in line with what God wants.

Money, and all the pretty things that money can buy, will not make us happy— not by itself. The old saw, Money won't buy you love, but just try getting some without any, not withstanding. Always remember: everything belongs to God. As his sons and daughters, we must follow his instructions. Grow a plan of action so that you can earn what you need to live on. Learn to spend less than you earn. And most important, avoid taking on debt of any kind. The surety and the interest on that debt places too much of a burden on even the best of incomes.

# *Biblical Livelihood*

-----◇◆◇-----

Deuteronomy 24:6—Do not take a pair of millstones—not even the upper one—as security for a debt, because that would be taking a person's livelihood as security.[12]

In the original Hebrew, the word for livelihood is nephesh, meaning soul or life. In some contexts it stands for the breath of life. Without a means to earn a living, we are only partially alive. That breath of life that we need to survive in this society is missing.

Leviticus 19:12—Do not swear falsely by my name and so profane the name of your God. I am the LORD.

Leviticus 19:13—Do not defraud or rob your neighbor. Do not hold back the wages of a hired worker overnight.

Leviticus 19:14—Do not curse the deaf or put a stumbling block in front of the blind, but fear your God. I am the LORD.

In Leviticus, God tells Moses and Moses tells the people a long series of business ethics. When you tell someone you are going to pay him so much for the work he does, you pay him. When you agree to work for a given length of time, you do that. Furthermore, you are humane to the people around you. You don't poke fun at people's infirmities, or make it any harder for them than it already is.

I invest my money, and more importantly, I earn my money by applying Biblical principles not only to my life but to my businesses. A few people have come to me saying they would like to be a business partner with me. But I don't want to take their money as those people are committing adultery and doing other things that have me feeling they would not have a good influence on my business, because they are not praying and paying attention to what God wants in their lives. If I were to let those people invest in my business when they are not clear with God, then my business could suffer. I don't want to take that risk.

The bankers make their money out of greed. We cannot take the bankers and their greed out of our money, but we can let God take the greed out of our hearts. I know plenty of people who earn well over $150 thousand a year, but they can't save

___

12    NIV

even $10 thousand. They are too much into what they can buy right now. Saving for an emergency—and since when can we live life without emergencies?—or to help their children go to school, or so they have something to live on when they retire almost never crosses these people's minds. We don't need to be spending $400 on our hair every two months at the salon. We don't need to get the most expensive car on the lot, and we surely don't need to build up credit card debt so high we'll be paying on it till the day we die. As I said, we cannot change the way bankers manufacture and control money, but we can take the greed out of the ways we get and spend money. I like to donate money to good organizations to help as many people as I can. These organizations base their activities on spiritual values, in order to meet real needs within the communities where they are located.

My mother told me story of a Russian immigrant who stood on street corners in NYC raising money. He was a very good hustler, and he was able to raise $1.5 million. This immigrant took his money to City Hall, trying to find the right place to put it where it would heolp poor people. Our immigrant was taken to Mayor Bloomberg's office, where he told the mayor he had been raising that money to help the homeless people. Everywhere he went there were homeless people, and he wanted to do something that would help. The mayor asked him how much of that money he wanted to keep for himself. Our immigrant said, "Nothing. I want to give it to help the homeless people." I pray that this money really was spent to help some homeless people get off the street and build better lives.

Doing work that helps other people and supports yourself and your family is spiritual. Yes, my business has been successful. I lived in New York City, which is known for being a hard city to make it. I started out driving a van to take children who live near the United Nations building safely to school and bring them home at the end of the day. It was much better for the children than having to go to and from school on public transportation. Now I have a small fleet of vans and busses to take children to school and home again. I do not like to take credit for my business—it is God who guides everything I do. God showed me His plan for my business as well as his plan for my personal life.

God wants us to have good relationships within our communities. Taking the greed out of the ways we deal with money will go a long way towards developing good relationships within our communities.

# *Holy Relationships*

———◈———

Philippians

2:1—Therefore if you have any encouragement from being united with Christ, if any comfort from his love, if any common sharing in the Spirit, if any tenderness and compassion,

2:2—then make my joy complete by being like-minded, having the same love, being one in spirit and of one mind.

2:3—Do nothing out of selfish ambition or vain conceit. Rather, in humility value others above yourselves,

2:4—not looking to your own interests but each of you to the interests of the others.

2:5—In your relationships with one another, have the same mindset as Christ Jesus:

2:6—Who, being in very nature [a] God, did not consider equality with God something to be used to his own advantage;[13]

Chapter Two of Philippians speaks beautifully of the sorts of relationships we are expected to have with our families, our friends and our neighbors, the people in our churches and temples and our work associates. These relationships are all holy. They are life sustaining.

The entire New Testament is filled with the ideals Jesus gave to the world, concerning how we should treat the people around us. The one thing he taught his disciples above all others is to love God first and foremost.

Moses taught the Israelites, as they were wandering through the wilderness:

Love the Lord your God with all your heart, with all your soul, with all your strength. And these words I command you this day, will be upon your heart. You will diligently teach them to your children. You will speak them when you sit at home, and when you are traveling on your way, when you lie down, and when you rise up.[14]

---

[13]   NIV
[14]   Deuteronomy 6:5 - 7

We live in a sad world, where black children have to work twice as hard as most white children, just to stay out of trouble. Sometimes the best guidance we can find to help then through is to teach them to pray with an open heart, an open mind and love, for themselves, the people around them and for God. And to pray for strength and wisdom and the ability to help each other. When your heart is open to love, you glimpse the purity—that spark of God, which is in every one of us.

When your spirit is that open and pure, it is too easy to ignore the anger and lies that so many people carry around with them. Sometimes I feel that having a pure spirit leaves me vulnerable to the enemy. We must develop our wisdom, so that we can soothe the anger we encounter.

I see so many people walking around, trying to hide their pain behind their smiles. Their pain is so close to the surface that if you say something kind to them, they break down and cry. Believe me, I know what it is to hurt. I lost two babies from sudden infant death syndrome. Losing those children was among the harshest things I have ever experienced. It was like losing an arm or a leg. Their deaths came at a time when I was seriously questioning who and what I was, and where I stood within my family, my community and with myself. Brandon and I had been looking forward to having those babies. Reading self help and motivational books did help, but it was through my love of God that I learned how to love myself, and how important it is to take care of myself. If I don't take care of me, I cannot take care of my children or my husband, and I truly cannot help anyone else.

When my babies died I blamed myself. Remember, by the time I was fifteen-years-old, I'd already had four or five abortions. When I married Brandon and then lost those babies, I was certain something must be wrong with me, if not physically then spiritually, which was making my babies die.

I had to learn how to love myself, before I could begin to turn my life around. Sometimes, loving yourself is the hardest thing to do, especially if you were unlucky to have parents who taught you that you weren't good enough, and that you don't deserve any of the good things in life. A lot of people have been unlucky that way. It can take years to learn how to deal with guilt, and put it in its place. If your parents told you nasty things like that when you were growing up you got hurt pretty deeply. You were hurt worse than you would have been if people had said those things to you when you were grown up. After that kind of abuse, it takes prayer and patience to learn how to love yourself.

Our society and our religions teache women that they should always place other people first and treat themselves as though they are less than human. It might be possible for the truly enlightened person to do this and not go crazy. But the rest of us can only begin to learn how to love other people by first learning how to love ourselves. And anyone, man or woman, who has been told from the time he was little that he was worthless, will not know how to love anyone at all.

A wise person once said that for women, the old saying; Do unto others as you would have others do unto you, should be turned around. For women it should say; Do unto ourselves as we would do unto others. In other words, while you are helping your brother or your sister through a rough time, don't forget to be good to yourself. One of the first things students in nursing schools are taught is that the nurses must take care of themselves first, because a whole ward full of people is depending on those nurses to be strong and capable. Don't be a martyr. Once the martyr is dead, she can't do anything for anyone. When we truly know how to help each other, without taking advantage of each other and putting each other down, the universe will be full of good things for all of us.

There is a story that a man called Rebbe Nachman told many years ago. It's about a prince who got it into his head that he was worthless. Maybe he didn't know how to act like a prince, and maybe his teachers told him he was too stupid and clumsy to be a real prince. For whatever reasons, our prince decided that if he couldn't feel like a real prince, he would be a turkey. He took off his clothes, crawled under the dining table and insisted he would eat only the crumbs that fell to the floor.

Now, his father the king was deeply upset. He had all kinds of wonderful things for his son to do and to learn, but if the boy were going to insist on living under the table like a turkey, his father didn't see how he could give him any of those things. This king called all the wise men in the country and begged them to please help get his son out from under that table.

Many wise men came. They stared at the boy and hemmed and hawed. Perhaps the king should feed his son seeds and scraps from the kitchen. Or maybe he should put him out in the chicken coop. The king didn't want to do any of that. Some of the wise men said his father should force the boy out and insist that he behave like a prince. The king said he had tried that, but his son crawled right back under the table. Maybe the boy could be enticed out with all the wonderful things—a beautiful princess no less—to make him want to be a prince again. The king wasn't sure about bringing a princess in to see his son hiding under the table with no clothes.

But there was one wise man who said, "I believe I can help bring your son back to you, but I will need time to do this."

The king said, "I give you three months," and he went to bed.

The wise man took off his clothes and crawled under the table with the prince. The prince stopped pecking at the floor long enough to eye the wise man up and down and said. "What are you doing here?"

"I'm a turkey, just like you." The wise man began to peck the floor for crumbs, to show the prince that he was also a turkey.

Several days went by. Summer was coming to an end and the nights were chilly. The wise man called one of the servants over and said, "I'm cold. Bring me a shirt and some pants."

The servant brought him his clothes and the wise man put them on. The turkey prince reared back on his heels and flapped his arms. "I thought you were a turkey!"

The wise man merely shrugged his shoulders. "Turkeys can wear clothes."

So, the prince asked the servant to bring him some clothes too, and the wise man and the prince continued pecking for crumbs on the floor, clucking over good ones and squabbling every now and then over an especially good crumb.

Days went by. The king had a feast prepared to celebrate the changes of the seasons. Many fine guests came. The table was laid out with wonderful food, roasts, fruit from far away, fish, cream sauces and nuts. The smells were tantalizing. Everyone sat down to eat. The prince had not had a full meal in many weeks, and he was hungry. He looked up longingly at the table and said, "I hope they drop some good crumbs tonight."

Our wise man winked at him, crawled out from under the table and sat down to eat with the guests.

The wise man looked down at the prince and said, "Turkeys can eat at the table too."

So, the prince crawled out from under the table and sat down with the wise man, the king and all the other guests. Needless to say, the king was overjoyed.

There are many ways to look at this story. A very simple moral to this tale could be, even us turkeys can eat from the table that God has prepared for us. This was the message that Jesus did everything he could to teach us. Some people would say that the only way to really help someone is by getting in there with him, to experience the same problems he has. Jesus certainly did that when he came to Earth as a man of flesh and blood and was finally tortured to death. During his life, He was the greatest example of what a good man can be. He did all he could to help the people around him. That was the message that Jesus did everything he could to teach us.

One of my clients, a woman who appears to have some things to learn about children and values, sent her six-year-old daughter to school in an expensive fur coat. The little girl was sitting with her friends on the bus, messing around, as children will, and her coat got torn.

Her mother was incensed. She wanted to sue the woman whose daughter had torn her little girl's coat. I would not give her the name of that woman, as I believe that her fighting with that other little girl's mother would do no one any good. Instead, I offered to pay to have the little girl's coat mended. This woman was not satisfied with that. She wanted to fight instead.

A few days later, the Department of Transportation came to my door to find out what was going on. I told the fellow that Billy Bing was my inspector and I have a good relationship with him. What did this inspector want? He couldn't be interested in whether a child's coat got torn on the way home from school. The DOT does not get involved in personal affairs. The woman still wanted to sue, so I had to tell her she had twenty-four hours to find another bus service for her little girl. I will not permit that sort of trouble on my buses.

You see, the relationships we have with our families, our friends, the people in our churches and temples, our work associations, are all holy. When we make mistakes in the way we treat people, we have to live with those mistakes. If we're smart, we learn so that we don't make those mistakes again. The entire New Testament is filled with advice on how we should treat the people around us.

Relationships with friends, neighbors and family can be wonderful. However it is too easy to take them for granted, and lose sight of how blessed we are to have good relationships with the people we care about. And then we come in contact with someone who is hurting because the relationships he cares about most, those with parents, spouses and children, are too painful to be endured.

When let a sick relationship continue for too long, putting up with negative energy from the other person, we begin to give out negative vibes. It goes with being human. That is when the relationship should end, or at least laid to rest, until people have let go of their hard feelings. And most relationships go sour because communication breaks down.

1 Timothy 5:1—Rebuke not an elder, but entreat him as a father, and the younger men as brethren.

1 Timothy 5:2—The elder women as mothers; the younger as sisters, with all purity.

These verses show the most basic ideal of good communication. Treat the other person with respect, a you would an elder or a brother, and show him that you care.

Sometimes we cannot figure out how to communicate with each other, even when we know we all speak the same language. Books and more books have been written about how to communicate with our family, and with our coworkers on the job, how to be assertive, how to avoid disputes, how to understand the body language of the person who is talking to you, and how to project confidence in who you are and what you have to say. There is no one formula that always works in every situation. Sometimes our best intentioned words will bring up terrible memories in the person we want to comfort.

When God brought down the Tower of Babel in Genesis 11:1-9, He not only muddled communication between people who speak different languages, but He muddled it between brothers and sisters and husbands and wives and friends and neighbors. Your experiences and memories shpe the wya you interpret what people say to you and how they acto twoards you. And your experiences are not the same as the person sitting beside you. Harper Lee, in To Kill a Mockingbird wrote; You never really know a man until you understand things from his point of view; until you climb into his skin and walk around in it. It was the Cherokee Indians who said, Don't judge a man until you have walked a mile in his shoes. Never mind the fact that you'll then be a mile away from him and you'll have his shoes! The object is to understand why he feels and acts the way he does. Understanding is the first step towards letting go of your anger, and letting go of your anger is the first step towards forgiving. If you can understand where your brother is coming from, it is much easier to find the words that would mean something to him.

Shrot of that, you pray for the wisdom to be able to speak words that will carry the love you have for the other person. And remember; it has been said that when your heart breaks, it opens up so that you can love more deeply, and laugh with greater feeling.

# Faith and Prayer

Psalm 145

A psalm of praise. Of David.

1 I will exalt you, my God the King;
I will praise your name for ever and ever.

2 Every day I will praise you
and extol your name for ever and ever.

3 Great is the LORD and most worthy of praise;
his greatness no one can fathom.

4 One generation commends your works to another;
they tell of your mighty acts.

5 They speak of the glorious splendor of your majesty—
and I will meditate on your wonderful works.

6 They tell of the power of your awesome works—
and I will proclaim your great deeds.

7 They celebrate your abundant goodness
and joyfully sing of your righteousness.

8 The LORD is gracious and compassionate,
slow to anger and rich in love.

9 The LORD is good to all;
he has compassion on all he has made.

10 All your works praise you, LORD;
your faithful people extol you.

11 They tell of the glory of your kingdom
and speak of your might,

12 so that all people may know of your mighty acts
and the glorious splendor of your kingdom.

13 Your kingdom is an everlasting kingdom,
and your dominion endures through all generations.
The LORD is trustworthy in all he promises
and faithful in all he does.[c]

14 The LORD upholds all who fall
and lifts up all who are bowed down.

15 The eyes of all look to you,
and you give them their food at the proper time.

16 You open your hand
and satisfy the desires of every living thing.

17 The LORD is righteous in all his ways
and faithful in all he does.

18 The LORD is near to all who call on him,
to all who call on him in truth.

19 He fulfills the desires of those who fear him;
he hears their cry and saves them.

20 The LORD watches over all who love him,
but all the wicked he will destroy.

21 My mouth will speak in praise of the LORD.
Let every creature praise his holy name
for ever and ever.[15]

Faith is the evidence of those things we hope for. When you live in your faith, trusting that the Lord is nearby, and that he does watch over those who love Him. Much of what you need to do will come to you, not only through conscious thought but through your God-given instincts. My favorite story about faith is in Luke 7:1-10. In this story, Jesus had just arrived in Capernaum, when the Jewish elders approached him to say that a Roman Centurion had begged them to ask Jesus to heal his slave. We tend to forget that Jesus was Jewish. This would explain why the Centurion appealed to the Jewish elders for help, when he wanted to see Jesus. The Centurion did not believe he was worthy to talk to Jesus personally or to have Jesus come into his home, for he was not Jewish. This centurion believed that all Jesus needed to do was say something would be so and it would be done, as Captain Lean Luc Picard

---

[15] NIV

would say, "Make it so." On hearing the Centurion's words, Jesus says, "I have not found so great faith, no, not in Israel." and of course, the servant was healed.

Everything boils down to faith—whether we have any, whether we don't. But more important than whether we have faith is where we put it. What do we believe in? Do you have faith in your job? With the economy the way it is, your job might not last. Do you have faith in your family? Fifty percent of the marriages in the United States end in divorce. Do you have faith in money? The more we learn about economics, the less any of us feel we can trust that. Do you have faith in yourself? That is a beginning, though some days we don't function as well as we might. We make mistakes, we grow old and we get sick.

What do we really trust will be there for us when we need it? It finally boils down to the fact that we need to make peace with the Ruler of the Universe, for that is all that truly is.

Faith in God is powerful. In Matthew 17:20, Jesus tells his disciples that if their faith were even as small as a grain of mustard, it would be enough to move mountains. Without faith, there is nothing. When we don't have faith that the source of all power is there for us, we don't have much of anything.

Some of us don't like to talk about Jesus because of the ways His name has been misused and misrepresented in Sunday Schools and other such places. But we still search for something that is bigger and stronger than ourselves, something that will guide us through both the horrific and the good things that come our way. Call it what you will, the inner light, the still, small voice within, the eternal spirit, or even simply, the Holy Name. It adds up to something I've said before, and I'll say it again. Every religion is different on the outside, but when you scrape off the layers and get down to the level of the spirit, they are all the same. We begin by having faith that there is something—the great creative force of the universe—that wants us to find Him. Some people say that God plays hide-and-seek with us—that He is here, there and everywhere we are, just waiting for us to turn around and open our eyes so that we can see Him.

Yes, it's true. I don't care for a lot of churches. Too many preachers have forgotten who they are supposed to serve and what it means to serve their congregations. The church is there to help the sick and the poor. Preachers should not beg money from people who don't have enough to live on, even though those people are often the most generous. They are the ones who know what it means to have to do without. Too many preachers are more interested in collecting money to build larger and fancier churches that don't get used for much, so they can prove to the world that what they do has value. Too many preachers are simply mixed-up people who have forgotten where true value lies. Somehow they have come to believe that their greatest value lies in dunning their parishioners for more money.

I have seen ministers put all their energy into courting the wealthy members of their congregations, trying to keep those people happy so that they will give more money, while forgetting about the rest of the people in their congregations who they are supposed to serve. These preachers often treat their wives and families as though they were second class citizens—as though they didn't count in the great scheme of things, while the poorer members of their congregations hardly exist for them. This is not the way it is meant to be. The Bible says a minister is to love his church as he would love his wife, and that he is to love his wife as he loves himself. See? It all comes back to knowing how to love yourself.

I am saying these things here, so that you don't get turned off to religion.

You don't have to go to a big church and pray kneeling down in front of a fancy cross for your prayers to reach heaven—though it is wonderful when you do find a minister who is able to touch your heart and soul. When you do find such a minister, you cherish that person and what he or she has to say. But church is really about community, and some of us search for years before we find the church community where we feel at home. When a church community takes joy in doing things together and takes care of each other, it's like a second family. There you can learn what it really means to love one another, and that is what the Kingdom of Heaven is really about. Ministers and preachers can come and go. Get strong with your community and together with them, learn what it means to love God.

It doesn't matter whether you see God as that woman who sits on high—laughing at you every time you try to do something that doesn't work out—or as a gentle parent who would gladly open your eyes to see what is right and good for you and the people around you, if you would only listen and see. In the Book of Proverbs, King Solomon says, "Six things the Lord hateth, and the seventh his soul detesteth."

First on that list is a proud look. This is a look that goes beyond self-respect. It is the expression of kings and commanders who have forgotten what it is to serve.

Second is a lying tongue. In some cultures, lying is acceptable. But for those who build a strong connection with the Eternal Spirit, lying hurts. It hurts not only the person who tells the lie, but it hurts the person who listens to it and believes it. It goes beyond that as well, hurting the person who was lied about.

Third is the slaughter that sheds innocent blood. We know how horrible war is, and we know there was a tremendous amount of blood spilled during our history as slaves. We are still reeling from that.

Fourth, is a heart that devises wicked plots. In other words, taking delight in finding ways to hurt innocent people. We are not in the positions of power that our bankers are, but we are able to spread good wherever we go.

Fifth; Feet that are swift to run into mischief. There is virtue in jumping into activities that you know will be helpful for those around you. But when you are confronted with activities that will cause pain for others, it is time to stop and pray.

Sixth: A deceitful witness that uttereth lies. Courts, hearings and trials are all too common for most of us. We know the pain that is inflicted when someone lies at such a hearing, knowing their lies will put one of us in prison.

We know how destructive it is to our children when their teachers lie about what they are and are not able to do. For years, my daughter's teacher insisted she did not know how to read, when in fact, my little girl loves to read, and she understands what she reads.

And number seven on this list: Him that soweth discord among his bretheren. We call this playing one person against another. I know several people who are very good at doing this. Mother-in-law jokes aside, we all know elderly women who entertain themselves by going to one of their children and telling lies about their sisters and brothers, and then going to another one of their children to tell more lies about the sisters and brothers, starting wonderful fights among their children. Do these old ladies laugh about the pain they cause? Is watching their children squabble about things that aren't even real more exciting than watching the soap operas on television? Mastering our tongues can be difficult as we must constantly listen to what we are saying, and learn to think before we open our mouths.

I have seen members of some church congregations spread bad words about people. This creates evil. In business we call it back stabbing. It hurts the people you are working with, making them want to hurt you back.

Spreading hurtful gossip can be one of the most potent ways to hurt a person, even if what you are saying is true. Be very careful about what you say about other people. We know some black sisters who delight in tearing down the businesses other black people are working to establish. They aren't above calling state inspection agencies with their lies about those businesses, in order to force them to close. Why do we hurt each other that way? Is it because we have been kicked down so often it hurts every time we see anyone make a go of their lives?

In Paul's epistle to the Galatians, Galatians 5:19, the list of sins includes adultery, fornication, strife, wrath, envy, murder and drunkenness, among other things. Saint Paul said that people who commit those sins will not inherit the Kingdom of God. We try not to do those things, in order to build good relationships with our families and good business relationships. But these are all the negative things we try not to do when we take in God's vision for our lives. What about the positive things that we should do? As the rabbi once said, when asked to explain the meaning of the Five Books of Moses, Genesis, Exodus, Leviticus, Numbers and Deuteronomy, while standing on one foot. The rabbi said, "Do unto others as you would have them do unto you. The rest is commentary." I could go on for pages and pages about how I believe people should lead their lives. Still, it is up to each of us to do what we are ready to do.

Benjamin Franklin joined the Quaker religion when he was a young man. The Quakers believe in promoting peace. Their members have a reputation for being non-combatants during times of war. In Ben Franklin's day, young men did not consider themselves dressed if they did not have their swords buckled round their hips. But the Quakers did not wear weapons. Franklin was concerned about this. He did not feel he could give up wearing his sword. The elder of his community told him, "Thee will stop wearing thy sword when thou art ready."

We don't stop sinning overnight. It's a step-by-step process. We stop doing destructive things and learn to do helpful things, as the spirit moves us. And it is prayer that opens us to what the Quakers call that still, small voice within, and what other Christians call the Holy Spirit.

Prayer can take many forms. There is the story of the old Jew, standing with his congregation at that time of year when all good Jews spend an entire day together, fasting and praying for forgiveness of their sins. One elderly man was thinking about all the things that had happened that year; how his wife had died of cancer, and how his son was in prison, and his daughter had been injured in a traffic accident. Then he thought of the troubles his neighbor had experienced, and the wars being fought overseas. He stood with the rest of the congregation, wondering why God would permit such bad things to happen to people whom he knew did their best to be good. Those things made no sense to him at all. At last he said, "Dear Lord, if you forgive me for the small jokes I have played on you, I will forgive you for the big jokes you have played on me and the people I love."

The man standing beside him turned to him and said, "You're being too easy on God."

Lives are often destroyed by things that are beyond our control. Perhaps the beginning of prayer can be letting God know how angry you are. Tell him how you feel. Lay it all at His feet. Don't be afraid to say, "Where were you when my baby died? Where were you when you made my mother suffer so much? This may be the beginning of a much needed conversation between you and God.

Rabbi Harold Kushner wrote a book called, When Bad Things Happen to Good People, in response to the grief he experienced after his son died at the age of fourteen of the genetic disorder, progeria. The rabbi prayed to God, what had his son ever done to deserve that cruel death? Of course, the answer was, nothing. Then he asked what he had done as a rabbi and as a human being to have to lose his son in that painful way. Isn't God supposed to be all-knowing and all-seeing? Couldn't He have prevented this death? And if He could have, why didn't He?

The answer for the rabbi is that bad things happen, even when you are doing everything you can to lead a good life. Bad things happen to good people, and they happen to people who don't care who or what they hurt, as long as they get what they want. It's like crossing a busy street. You might get hit by that semi barreling down the road, or, you might not. It's like playing the lottery—you might actually draw the winning number. Some people have quipped that going out to sea in a leaky boat. You can bail water all you want, but sooner or later that boat will sink. A few of you were born into families that were able to show you all the love they had, and to give you everything you needed. A lot of you were born into families that could not do those things. So, you learned different lessons at home.

However, as you grope your way through those long, dark tunnels of life, and everyone has experienced at least one long dark tunnel in his life, you may discover that the light you have been heading for isn't daylight at all, but a freight train bearing down on you. It is what you do about the situation that brings you closer to the angels. Do you pray and search for God's guidance? Do you give up and let the train crush you under its wheels? Do you try to help other people who are caught in the same situation with you? Or, do you crush them under your feet, in your attempt to get out of there? It is the choices you make, the things you do with your lives, that mark the difference between God-loving women and men, and people you may not want to know. It is the wisdom and compassion you grow, as you follow the teachings of Jesus, and those who are religious for show.

You see, there are no guarantees. When you get knocked down, you pick yourself up, dust yourself off and keep on going. And while you're at it, pray. Pray when you are alone. Get together with friends to pray, and pray with yor congregation at church.

Sometimes I feel like I am the only person in the world who is serving God. When was the last time you stopped at a church or a temple to pray? It gets lonely following God the way I do. When you lose sight of God, you lose sight of your destiny.

# Biblical Family Relationships

Genesis 29:5—And he said unto them, Know ye Laban, the son of Nahor? And they said, We know him.

Genesis 29:6—And he said unto them, Is he well? And they said, He is well, and behold, Rachel, his daughter, cometh with the sheep.

This continues the Jacob and Esau story. As you know, after Jacob and his mother cheated Esau out of their dying father's blessing, Jacob feared for his life. Wouldn't Esau take revenge? Jacob dashes off towards the country of his Uncle Laban. Now, we know that Jacob and his mother are not above doing a bit of conniving in order to get what they want. However, it may appear that Jacob has fallen from the frying pan into the fire. You see, Uncle Laban is even better at conniving that Jacob and his mother are. First, of course, Jacob falls in love with his cousin Rachel, and will do nearly anything at all to win her as his bride. Laban takes him on as a helper on his farm, and Jacob does his best to out-wit the old man, as far as who ultimately owns the most sheep is concerned. However, when it comes time to wed Rachel, Laban, without a by—your-leave, tricks him into marrying the older daughter first. We don't know how the older daughter felt about being married to a man who has the hots for her younger sister, but we can guess. You see, some traits do run in families.

Just what are biblical family relationships? If you are not familiar with the scriptures, you have good reason to ask. And if you are familiar with the scriptures, you may feel you have even better reason to ask! We could start with Adam and Eve and that famous story about the serpent and the apple. Let's see . . . Adam and Eve were standing next to a particular tree, growing in the midst of the Garden of Eden. A serpent slithers down out of the leaves and offers Eve a taste from one of the fruits of that tree. We don't know that this fruit was definitely an apple as the original text merely calls it a fruit.

Eve says, "I can't eat it, for if I do I would surely die."

Adam just stands there. He doesn't say or do anything. The serpent persists and Eve at last tastes the fruit. She says it's good and she offers Adam some. He never says a word. He just takes the fruit and eats it.

Until they tasted this fruit, those two innocents did not know the meaning of good and bad. They had never experienced guilt. They try to hide themselves in robes patched together from the leaves growing in the garden. God passes through and calls them out. "What have you done?"

Adam speaks first. "We ate from the fruit of that tree. She made me do it."

Women have been taking the blame for everyone's problems ever since. Adam could have at least tried to stop the serpent from tempting Eve, but he didn't. when Eve offered him the apple, he didn't turn away or say he didn't want any—he just took that apple and ate it.

The story of Cain and Able begins with the conflict between two brothers and one inheritance—one blessing. Cain killed Abel, which was not a good idea, and had to pay for that act for the rest of his life.

The story of Jacob and Esau carries the theme of conflict between brothers a few steps further. Jacob's mother tells him he is the one who should receive his father's first blessing, before the old man dies. The angels had told her, when her sons were born, that her second son Jacob would be the son to father a great nation. So, she believed she was doing the right thing when she told Jacob he should deceive his father. Some Bible commentators go so far as to say that Jacob's father knew what was happening and went along with it.

Now Esau had been out hunting. He came in tired and hungry. He saw a pot of potash Jacob had been cooking over the fire. He said he was so hungry he would give up his inheritance for a bowl of that "red red," probably a mixture of red lentils and vegetables. Jacob gave him a bowl and held his brother to the bargain.

Jacob was a gardener and Esau was a hunter. Their mother knew that her husband loved the offerings of his first born son—the roasted meats—better than he liked the offerings of his second son—the fruits and grains harvested from the fields. So, she has the younger boy dress up in furs so the old man will think he is the older brother. Jacob goes into the old man's room with a bowl of meat stew.

While the father lay dying, the mother dressed her second son in sleaves of fur, to make her husband think he was Esau. Then, she sent him in with a plate of roasted meat, and told him to ask for his father's blessing. Some people believe that the father really did know it was Jacob and not Esau standing before him, and that he went along with the deception. Perhaps he really wanted to give his blessing to the younger son.

Once his father has given him his blessing, and Esau realized what had happened, Jacob ran away. He spent years living in fear that his brother might kill him. Remember Cain and Abel? That story was very similar, except that Cain did kill Abel.

All of us make mistakes. It's part of being human. But, we get up again and try to do better. There is an old story about God and the Angels in heaven. The angels have a debate with God, saying, "Why do you put so much attention into those humans—they do such horrible things to each other? Aren't we perfect?"

God considers them and says, "Yes, you were made perfect. It is impossible for you to be anything but perfect. On the other hand, humans are a bundle of contradictions. They have to keep on trying to reach perfection. And when they come even close to perfection, it is time to rejoice."

That is what makes us special. We can be breathtakingly horrible. Greed and lust, combined with a lack of reverence for human life compel many people to torture and to kill, and to not care about the grief they create in the lives of others. But then, we can turn around and begin to approach the angels in perfection.

We can learn how to lead the life God wants us to lead. It is when we struggle to do what we know He wants that we approach the perfection of the angels. The parables Jesus told us are all about how we should be with our families and our work associates and our neighbors.

Family is the basis for all the relationships in our lives, including our business relationships, the relationship we have within our communities and the relationship we have with God. Maintaining good family relationships can be hard. Everyone knows it is easier to take care of your neighbors when they take care of you. Nobody wants to be held responsible for things they have done wrong. For instance, my niece, who is otherwise intelligent, made arrangements to move into a new apartment in New York City. Unfortunately, the lease on her old apartment ran out before she could get the key for her new apartment. Her new landlord was away on holiday for a few days, so she was stuck. She made one bad decision, though. She moved into my apartment without telling me. If she had called to tell me what her problem was, I would have been happy to let her stay there for a few days. As it was, I did not learn she was in there until a friend of mine told me someone was living in my apartment. So, I called her. I have to admit I was in a huff. "I want you gone. No. This isn't about money. If you had thought I wanted money, you would have called me. I never gave you permission to just move in whenever you wanted."

Several years before that, I helped her dad. I showed him how to start a transportation company so that he could take care of his family. It's sad, what my niece did, because now I don't feel so good about her father. I don't feel as though I can trust him the way I did. But sometimes, that is the way it is with family.

Things happen. Somebody does or says something that you don't like, and then you feel it's all over with that person. Things can get so bad you want that person out of your lives. Abusive husbands and abusive parents fall into that category. People who habitually lie also land there. You want to feel you can trust the people who are close to you.

Whenever someone I know, who has not been honest with me, comes to me saying she wants to work with me, I say, "Forget it. I can and do forgive you, but I cannot let myself be mistreated by you again." I love all my family. I walk out on limbs for them. But the minute they take advantage of me, I feel as though they have no respect for me. I guess I am my father's daughter in more ways than one.

All of us need to learn to pay good attention to the members of our families. That does not mean we give them everything they say they want. It does mean we listen to what they have to say. It means we take time to be with them. I know, many of you work two jobs, and some of you even work at three jobs, just to keep a roof over your head and food on the table for your children. So any time at all that you can be with your family is precious. Let your children know that you like being with them. Saying a little prayer with your children, or even a simple blessing, before you all have to dash off to work and school, can mean a whole lot to them and to you. If you can sit down with them every day to share a meal and to give thanks for what you do have, do it. But don't kick yourself if you cannot be with your family every day. Sometimes we have to find creative ways to show our families that we care about them.

I am raising my daughter to know what it means to be faithful to a man. That means she knows she can't start another relationship till she is out of the first one.

If she is not finished with the first relationship and she wants to be connected to something higher than herself, then she is not ready to start another relationship. I'm teaching her that being true to her man is only a small part of it. It means that every day, in one way or another, we show him that we love him. It means being patient with him, even when he doesn't do what we would like. It means respecting what he believes, even if we don't agree with him. And it means giving both him and yourself the encouragement to grow as human beings, adults and business people.

My husband introduced me to one of his friends. I'll call this friend Bob. Bob's mistress and their child were with him the day I met him. Now, my husband, Brandon, and I were supposed to go on a fishing trip with Bob and his wife. But once I had seen Bob with his mistress, I didn't want to have to face his wife. It felt like blood on my conscience, blood from the lies Bob had been telling his wife.

Now, it was obvious to me that Bob was embarrassed that I had seen him with his mistress, so this was not some sort of open marriage that he and his wife had agreed to. The problem for me was that I could not be with Bob's wife and not talk about what her husband was doing, and I couldn't' be with her and talk about it. I don't do things like that unless the woman comes to me for advice.

As Black people in the United States, we have been robbed, over and over again. I would have to write another book to even begin to talk about our families being brought over here as slaves, and another book again to describe what the Ku Klux Klan has done to us and the laws used to keep us living as slaves. Those things hurt the white people, because they create a stain on their consciences that will take generations to clean away, but they really hurt the Black people, who have to live with being treated like we aren't quit human. It hurt our parents, it hurts us, and it hurts our children.

We are suffering now because the good factory jobs have been sent overseas until there is no work in this country for 30 to 40 percent of the entire population; black, white or brown. Young men and women coming out of college with degrees, wind up working at places like Walmart and McDonalds, for little more than minimum wage. And they still have their college debts to pay. Most of the factories in this country are now prison factories. Nike Sneakers and Sylvania light bulbs, as well as nearly all the military equipment made in this country, as well as auto parts, fabric and clothing come out of prison factories. Prisoners cannot go on strike, and they cannot go on vacation. They get paid between twenty-three cents and a dollar fifteen an hour. Their labor is far less expensive than it would be to hire people who are not prisoners to do that same work. The United States has 25 percent of the world's prisoners and only 5 percent of the world's population. Prison factory owners are bribing judges across the country to sentence more people to prison, and keep them there longer. Prison labor has its roots in slavery. After the 1861-1865 Civil War, a system of "hiring out prisoners" was introduced in order to continue the slavery tradition. Freed slaves were charged with not carrying out their sharecropping commitments (cultivating someone else's land in exchange for part of the harvest) or petty thievery—which were almost never proven—and were then "hired out" for cotton picking, working in mines and building railroads. From 1870 until 1910 in the state of Georgia, 88% of hired-out convicts were Black. In Alabama, 93% of "hired-out" miners were Black. In Mississippi, a huge prison farm similar to the old slave plantations replaced the system of hiring out convicts. The notorious Parchman Plantation existed until 1972.[16]

The Zero Tolerance policies have spread from one school district to another, and are now instituted in 91 percent of the schools across the country. Zero Tolerance means that no act that could be considered violent is permitted in school. What it means is that a five-year-old child, who points a finger at his playmate and says bang, is immediately expelled from school. He is then carted out of the school, in handcuffs, with a policeman on each side, taken to the station and questioned about whether he wants to kill his classmates. That child then has a permanent police record, and is on the fast track from school to prison. This is exactly what the prison factory owners want. These policies are directed against black children far more than they are against other children.

What does this do to our sons? What our husbands and fathers went through was bad enough, but what our sons will experience in school and prison may be far worse.

One of my girl-friends called me to say she had a problem. She has a good job, and she's used to telling people what to do when she's at work. She earns enough to keep her family comfortable. But she was crying to me, "Aunty Bessie, what can I do to help my husband feel like a man? I love him, and I want him to know that he can be responsible for his family."

We began by praying, and I soon realized that my husband had never had to pay the bills, or make sure his family was fed. My Brandon had always worked, but I had been the one who made sure the bills were paid and our children went to good schools. I had simply stepped in and done those things, and he had never had to think about them.

Well, the good Lord told me it was time I stepped back and let Brandon take care of those things. Besides, I have my non-profit to take care of, and that will keep me busy for a long time. The best way to help a man grow up, may be to let him take responsibility for his family. Maybe it is time we gave our men and ourselves permission to be husbands and wives in the real sense of those words. My brothers, even though they each spent sixteen years in prison—too much time for any man to be locked away—are good men. Not only that, they worship the ground their wives walk on, and they make sure their families have what they need.

Our parents, bless their souls, came out of homes that were less than perfect. Often, the woman didn't know where the daddy to her children was, because he had run off, or was in prison. Sometimes she wasn't sure who the daddy was. She had to figure out how to take care of her children by herself. Most of the time, she just barely scraped by. It's never easy to pull your life together when you don't have the resources to make it work. By the time our parents had us, the ideal of Mom, Dad and two and a half children (I'm not sure where that half child was supposed to come from) was long gone. They did what they could, and some of us got pretty messed up. And if we were lucky, we managed to figure out what the real message was, and where it was coming from. The best way to begin to put your life in order is to look to see what God wants of you.

---

[16]    http://www.globalresearch.ca/the-prison-industry-in-the-united-states-big-business-or-a-new-for m-of-slavery/8289 March 14, 2013

I was at a book launch party for one of my girlfriends. All kinds of people were there. One of the girls, I'll call her Laura, gave me this nice, promotional T-shirt. We got to talking, and something told me she was pregnant. It wasn't as though her tummy showed. She just had this aura about her that made me think she was growing a baby. Call it my sixth sense, or call it God telling me it was so. When I said she looked pregnant, she said, "Oh my God! How can you tell?"

A few months later, I wanted to pick up some T-shirts like the one I'd got at the convention. I called the company that made them and it turned out that Laura was one of the owners of this company, importing cotton T-shirts from Peru. She called me right back. "Hi, Aunt Bessy."

I was excited to hear her voice. "How are you? When is the baby due?"

She was almost into tears. "Oh, Aunt Bessie, don't do this to me. I had an abortion."

"Aren't you married?"

I have one son that isn't my husband's. He helped me raise him."

I was disappointed to hear that she had chosen to have an abortion. She asked if we could talk later. When she did call back she said, "Aunty, I don't want you to think bad of me."

"I think you'd be a good mom." "No, I live a good life. I work for a hedge fund. My husband left." "Don't you think it could be because of the abortion? That could be a hurting situation."

I have been talking to her, nearly every morning at six o'clock, ever since. She tries to keep up her guard, play it safe so no one can hurt her. She helped me get a million dollars to put into my non-profit. She wants to do whatever she can to help. God put her in my path.

We pray and keep our hearts open to what the Good Lord tells us, and we do what we are ready to do. Everybody makes mistakes, and we all have burdens from our past that we have to overcome. I do what I can to help Laura find a better way, and maybe find her way back to her husband, and Laura sees what she is ready to see, and understands what she is able to understand. She still hurts.

I like to live my life in a spirit of submission to the word of God. I go to the scriptures for my inspiration. Proverbs 18:22 says, He who finds a wife, finds a good thing and gains favor from the Lord. I live my life so that I am that sort of wife. Everyone needs a good friend to talk to, someone who will remind them of the way they should be taking their lives, because it is so easy to lose sight of who you are serving. Ideally, husbands and wives should help each other this way, though we cannot expect that our mates will always be there for us.

I was sitting at a restaurant eating my sandwich, when this man came up to me and told me his whole life story. He was a white man who had married a black woman from another country, but his wife left him when he brought her over to the United States. I had to tell him that we must learn to wait on God. He is the one who picks out the husbands and wives for us. There is an old story that says God's greatest purpose is to find the right mate for each person. It may take years for Him to find that mate for us, and we may have a lot to learn about ourselves and our relationship with our neighbors and with God, before He shows us who that right person is. I feel as though I found the perfect man for my life. He may not be every woman's idea of perfection, but he suits my needs very well, and for years, I believed I suited his needs.

Brandon and I have had some very fine times together, and believe me, I have learned a tremendous amount, about life, and about myself and what I expect from the men around me. I am certain he has learned a lot, living with me. Still, it is time for Brandon and me to go our own ways. For the sake of our children, we'll do this peaceably, as friends. Perhaps at some future time, we will live together again as husband and wife, but for now, Brandon has some growing and learning to do, and I have my business to take care of. No, I won't tell you the old joke about the difference between men and bonds. Everyone knows that bonds mature, but can we all say that men do? I believe that Brandon can. In the meantime, I will be working on my business.

Waiting on God can mean doing things that most other people wouldn't understand. Laura told me that if I went to ten people and got together 250 thousand dollars for my non-profit, she could invest it and give me back 15 million on it. I called my accountant, who happens to be a lawyer, and ran her offer past him. He said the numbers didn't sound right. He wanted to know whether she was getting the money through acquisitions and mergers, and what his involvement might be, if he did give me the money for her to invest for me. He did not feel right about investing in her project without having more information.

I called her and she said, "I hate people! I'll email you the information and you can send it on to your accountant. I was doing this for you—not for him!"

"But we're asking him for a quarter of a million dollars!" I was beginning to feel like she was a scam artist. Then God showed me to slow down and stay on the assignment with her. People trust me because I keep working with them, even when so-called common sense would say that I shouldn't. I believe God put me in Laura's life to keep her together with her husband. I haven't met him, but I am sure he is a wonderful man. God is showing me what my work with her needs to be. I sat down and prayed. I decided that if I did take her up on her offer, I would owe him the two hundred fifty thousand. I prayed over and over again, "Lord, this is a lot of money."

It is interesting the ways in which our children reflect our ideals. My thirteen-year-old son is big on charity. He wants to help as many people as he can. A few weeks ago, my son spoke at a fund raising event and people were astonished over how well he spoke. He was the one who really inspired people there to open their wallets and write some checks. He talked about his grandfather who is seventy-one-years-old, and needs money for medications and other things like that.

If there is one thing my son knows, it is how to persuade people. They are often too terrified to open their mouths to tell you what they think. They find it extremely difficult to put down their little I-phones in order to put their attention into the people around them. But my son can get up in front of any group of people. He knows how to make you weep, and he knows how to make you laugh, and he knows how to make you open up your wallet. People come up to talk with him, and they forget that he is so young, because he has the wisdom of a man more than twice his age.

# Honesty

Job 10:14—If I sin, then thou markest me, and thou wilt not aquit me from mine iniquity.

Proverbs 20:17—Bread of deceit is sweet to a man, but afterwards, his mouth shall be filled with gravel.

It is too easy to forget what honesty means. Too many of us have been in prison, where to be honest, it wasn't particularly healthy to be honest about what you had or had not done, or about what you saw somebody else doing. The sad thing is, we would hardly make it through this world, if we didn't believe we could trust the people around us not to be hurtful and not to take advantage of us. It all comes back to the Golden Rule—Do unto others as you would have them do unto you. That means that if you want to be treated with respect at work, then you have to treat your co-workers with respect, and you have to treat yourself with respect. If you want to teach your children to tell the truth, then you have to be truthful with them, and you have to be truthful with yourself and not lie to yourself, or kid yourself that what you do is right when you steal from your friends, or hurt someone you care about.

I am the sort of friend who reminds you of the things you would rather forget. So, it puzzles me sometimes why my friends keep coming back for more. I don't mince words when I see someone has done something that is not right.

I was visiting someone's home with one of my girlfriends. She saw a pair of sunglasses that had been left on the table by the couch. Without a by-your—leave, she put them on her face, and wore them when we went out.

Months later, she came to me, saying she would like to invest in my business and work with me. I told her she had better make closure with that woman about the sunglasses she took, before she thought about working with me. You see, good business relationships, just like good family relationships and relationships with your friends are based on trust. No matter what sort of contract you sign, you have got to be able to trust that the other person will keep his end of the deal, or you're sunk. I cannot have people working with me who do not live by the Ten Commandments, and I teach my children at home to live by them.

What we know as the Ten Commandments come out of Deuteronomy 5:4-21. Deuteronomy shows Moses when he is a very old man. He knows that because of mistakes he has made, he will not be able to go into the Promised Land. The entire book of Deuteronomy consists of his last words to his people, as he stands with them at the River Jordan. He describes how he got them out of Egypt—that narrow place—and he describes all the things that happened as they passed through the wilderness. He announces who will be leading the Israelites, once they have crossed the Jordan. He dies at the end of this book.

The following verses from Chapter Five are his exhortation to the people to do and be an example to the other nations.

5:4 ~ I am the Lord your God, who brought you out of the land of Egypt, out of a house of serfs.

In other words; this is who I am and this is why you should worship me.

5:5 ~ You are not to have other gods beside my presence.

We know too many people who worship money. Now, money is a very good thing to have when it comes time to pay your rent and buy your groceries. And it is wonderful when you know how to earn what you need to live, and you are able to teach your children how to earn what they will need. But, to set it up as a god within your heart and worship it? All around us, we can see the destruction the worship of money brings, such as; the building up of ghettos that are anything but cheap to live in, and the sending of good paying jobs overseas and the building of prison factories here in the US, where prisoners are worked as slaves. These are the evils that the worship of money creates.

5:6 ~ You are not to make yourself a carved image of any form that is in the heavens above, that is on the earth beneath, that is in the waters beneath the earth.

It is this verse, along with a few others that speak against making graven images, that many religious people have interpreted to mean they should make nothing in the human image. The Old Order Amish will permt no photographs to be taken of themselves, and even the dolls they make for their little girls to play with do not have faces, as they believe such things would go against what the scriptures teach. And Muslims believe they should never draw or carve pictures of the human body.

This verse may be difficult to understand, as we call such carved images statues and when they're beautiful, we like to look at them and have them in our homes. There is nothing wrong with being an artist, and enjoying beautiful things. It is worshiping the statue, as though your god lived within that piece of carved wood or stone, that is wrong. Once upon a time many people believed that their god lived in a statue, or idol, and that praying to that carved image was as good as praying directly to God. If having a statue of Jesus or of Mary in your home helps you remember how you want to live your life, that's fine. But God doesn't live in those statues. God is all around us in everything we see, hear and touch—in everyone we meet. Don't try to keep Him confined to a statue. Doing that will make you crazy.

5:7 ~ And don't worship animals, or even the sun and the stars, for they will not answer your prayers either.

This verse says what it means. Life on this planet is holy. God put us on this earth so that we could enjoy it. But the fish in the sea, the birds in the sky and the four legged animals of this earth are not gods to be worshiped. They are here for us to take care of them, and to enjoy. But they are not our gods. Likewise, there is a tremendous lot we can learn of this earth and the sun and the stars, but they are not gods to be worshiped either.

5:8 ~ You are not to prostrate yourselves to them, you are not to serve them, for I the Lord your God am a jealous God, calling to account the iniquity of the fathers upon the sons to the third and to the fourth, of those that hate me.

This idea is repeated in Proverbs where it says: The sins of the fathers are visited upon the sons, into the third and fourth generation. No matter how you try to teach your children right from wrong, if you are not doing what you teach them is right, your children will see that, and they will not trust you. The things you do that you know are wrong do affect your children, more than you realize.

In other words, love all of creation, for God did make it and we are here to enjoy it and to take care of it, so that our children and their children may also have it to enjoy. But do save your worship for God, who made you, as well as the universe around you.

5:9 ~ But stay loyal to thousands of those that love me, of those that keep my commandments.

And as you love God and strive to be the person God wants you to be, God blesses you and your children. For he stays loyal to all those who love Him and kee his commandments.

5:10 ~ You are not to take up the name of the Lord your God for emptiness—for the Lord will not clear him that takes up His name for emptiness.

This verse is generally interpreted to mean that we should not swear. It may more properly mean that you should not say you are a good Christian, or Muslim, or Jew, when you are not. Saying that you believe in a religion, simply for show, to make people think well of you when you don't care at all about that religion, is committing a sin. Before we claim that we are among Abraham's children— because the followers of all three of these religions are Abraham's children. We must pray and to think what it means to love God and how this should affect our daily lives. Is religion something you only do when you go to church? If church is the place you go to show off, then something is wrong and you need to think about where you are at and why you are calling yourself a religious person. Religion must spring from deep within your heart and soul. It does not depend on getting dressed in your fanciest clothes on Sunday morning, so that everyone can see that you are the best dressed person in town. If your religion shows itself in your compassion for all the people around you, then you are not taking up God's name in vain.

5:11 ~ Keep the day of the Sabbath by hallowing it, as the Lord your God has commanded you.

Some verses out of the Old Testament say you will die if you do not keep the Sabbath. Everyone who has worked on Sunday, or Friday, or Saturday, or whichever day you hold as your Sabbath, scoffs at that idea. Those of us who run our own businesses work hard, and often find there simply are not enough hours in the day to get everything done. Those of us who work on somebody else's clock may work even harder. The Man demands a lot of us. Many of us don't have a choice—we have to work seven days a week. But it is wrong to make anyone do that. Sure, working seven days a week won't kill you outright, but it does put stress on your inner being, your soul and your health. It becomes hard to function around your children and the people you care about. We need the down-time to heal and to think about where we are, what we are doing, and how we could manage better. We need that time to pray and to communicate with God. On the seventh day, God rested and made that day holy. That line is from Genesis. It does not say how He rested. He may have been sleeping. He may have simply been sitting back and enjoying the fruits of His labor. It does say that He made that day holy and that we are to keep it that way. As we evolve as People of the Book and learn to love God, how we choose to keep the Sabbath may change. What is important is that we do things to make that day special, both for ourselves and for the people around us. I raise my children to understand and to know and to believe what Jesus said, because His words are the best guide I know for making my life whole and productive.

We can't change the family we were born into. We can't change where and when we were born. Those things God gave us because we had lessons to learn, or He wanted to test us in special ways. We cannot pick and choose the trials our parents laid on us when we were growing up, or whether we live in a society that prospers or a society that is being beaten down, but we can learn from those trials, and we can pick ourselves up, wherever we happen to be, and move as God wants us to.

As we grow, we do have choices. I choose to follow God's plan for my life. I choose to make sure that what I do, the Lord Jesus wants me to do. I know that the man I married is the man God chose for me. He meets my needs as no other man could. He has helped me to grow as a human being and I have helped him to grow.

Following God's plan for your life does not mean that everything you do will instantly prosper. Maybe you need to learn a few things about failure before you can succeed. No, following God's plan for your life means that your conscience can be clear and the influence you have on your family and friends will help lead them to God.

When you lead your life based on God's principles, letting God chose your mate and then raising your children to be faithful and honorable, your mate and your children will be there for you when you need them, because you were there when they needed you.

When we are feeling tight with hurt and anger, we don't want to let anyone enter our lives so fully that they might be able to get a real handle on how we think and feel. Sometimes we stay closed out of fear that if the other person really got to know us—warts and all—they would think we were pretty awful and they would treat us badly, or leave us.

The mate whom God has given us isn't going to do that. We can let him know all the things about us that are neither perfect or pretty, and he will love us not just in spite of those things, but because of them—because they make us human.

The same thing is true of you for the other person. When he bears his soul and tells you things about himself that maybe he has never told anyone else, you will treat him gently, with words of wisdom and forgiveness, for that is what intimacy is about. You look into me and I look into you, and together we see the God that dwells within, and know that our living and working together keeps the devil at bay.

But remember, no matter how perfect your man is, he cannot keep you happy. Nor, can you keep anyone else happy. It is up to each of us to find that place within as well as the energy within to make ourselves happy. Nobody can do it for us. But God can show us how. Possessing lots of stuff won't make you happy and giving lots of stuff to someone else won't make them happy either. No matter how much stuff you have and how perfect your family is, you can always find reasons to be miserable.

Two things we all have to learn. First, you must find that space within yourself where you can be contented, and then you have to get yourself off your duff to do something about whatever it is that is wrong in your life. Most important, keep your communication with God open, so that He can show you the best ways to do those things.

A few pages back I talked about the Seven Deadly Sins, and some verses in the Old Testament that say God hates liars. If the Golden rule says we must do unto others as we would have them do unto us, then the first thing we must be with others is honest.

Honesty comes in layers. We go back and forth between trying to be honest with other people and realizing that maybe we haven't been honest with ourselves. Some of us seldom try to be honest. I once heard someone say that in business dealings, you must be strictly honest. Because for your own survival, you need to show your business associates that they can trust you. You can accomplish a lot more when the people you work with trust you than when they do not. I cringed when this person went on to say that it is perfectly all right to tell members of your family anything you want, in order to get them to do what you want.

Let's be real. Honesty begins with yourself. Part of loving yourself is disciplining yourself, the way a good parent makes it easier for her child to do what is right than to go off and hurt himself or others. It always begins with being honest with yourself.

Some women feel as though it's OK to have affairs with any man who turns her on. This can too easily turn into having a series of one night stands. Women who permit that in their lives need to sit down and think, Is this really the way I want to lead my life? Some of these women have children at home. They need to look at their child and think, Does this baby need his mother to be having affairs with all kinds of men? Real honesty begins at home with yourself, extends out to yoru children and your husband, and expands from there to the rest of your family, your church family, and your business associates.

Integrity is an old-fashioned virtue. It means that you are what you say you are, and that when you say you will do something, you do it. It means being honest with yourself. If you know you have a problem with alcohol or drugs, then you don't keep those things in your home. If you know you have such a rough temper you could hurt your children, you talk about that anger with your friends, your minister, with a counselor, and with God. You ask for help, and you listen to what they have t say. [look up references to anger in new Terstament]

We all have a temper, and we al go through times when we want to say or do things that would do more harm than good. It's part of being human.

Having integrity means that you know you are not perfect, and taking care of yourself means that you do the best you can, to live the life God wants you to live. That is how you bring peace and fulfilment into your life.

# *Darkness*

---------⟨∘⟩---------

Day, night, darkness, light—these are opposites—one feeds the other. Without darkness, we would not have light. Seeds sprout in the dark, in the earth where they go through that miraculous change from being a hard little pellet that barely resembles a living thing, to a plant pushing its roots into the earth for its sustenance, and stretching its leaves up to meet the sun. it is better for us to sleep in a quiet and darkened room, for the darkness is healing. Our spirits need to stretch and relax from our daily cares as much as our bodies do.

The dark times in our lives are harder to explain. During those times when troubles lie so heavily on us that we lose any sense that God could be with us, we must remember that we have much to learn from these dark times. Psalms 139:7-12 say:

> Whither shall I go from thy spirit? Or whither shall I flee from thy presence? If I ascend up into heaven, though art there; if I make my bed in hell, thou art there.
>
> If I take the wings of the morning and dwell in the uttermost parts of the sea, even there shall thy hand lead me, and thy right hand shall hold me.
>
> If I say, surely the darkness cover me, even the night shall be light about me.
>
> Yea, the darkness hideth not from me, but the night shineth as the day; the darkness and the light are both alike to thee.

These words say it all. I could end this book right here and I would have said everything. We can no more hide from the God that made us than we can hide from ourselves. We see the world in terms of duality. Day/night. Me/him. Spirit/everything else. Recognizing that God is with us and in everything is to recognize that it is all one. The universe and everything in it is God. There is no separation from Him.

# *Faith*

Faith. I have been talking about faith all through these pages. When you get down to it, faith is the most important thing in your relationship with God. The first meaning for this word is loyalty, being trustworthy. Are you faithful to your promises? This is the first thing I ask when someone comes to me to say he wants to invest in my business and work with me. Is this person faithful to his promises? Will I be able to trust him when things get rough? Life does have a way of throwing a few curve balls at us when we least expect them. Being faithful means to be trustworthy, keeping faith and being faithful to yourself, so that you can have faith in others and in God.

If we are all made in the image of God, and the universe and everything in it was made by God, then isn't it up to us to treat everyone and everything in the universe, including ourselves, with the respect due to God? Faith is a two—way street. You have faith in God, and God has faith in you.

Philosophers have spent lifetimes debating what faith is, what it means to have faith and in what we should place our faith. What they have to say makes fascinating reading, if you like to wade through page after page of argument. The second meaning of faith is belief in what you cannot see. My belief in Jesus has given me strength to face all sorts of trials and to deal with all sorts of questions, many of which I described to you in the first part of this book.

Some people argue that Jesus never existed, and if he did, he died more than two thousand years ago. How could anything He said or did have any meaning in my life today? Well, I'll tell you: Jesus lives in my heart, and he lives in the hearts of everyone who believes in him. Every time we read those passages in Matthew, Mark, Luke and John about his crucifixion, he is crucified for us all over again. Every time we read those passages that describe his resurrection, He rises to life again for each and every one of us. And every time we read the stories he told, his parables, it is as though He is sitting in front of us, telling those stories to you and to me, just as he did for the people more than two thousand years ago. There are many translations of the Bible.

Pick the one you like best and read it. Spend some time every day, reading and thinking about what it has to say to you. Think about how those old, old stories apply to your life today. That old-time preacher Dwight Lyman Moody, used to say, "The preachers that this world needs most is the sermons in shoes that are walking with Jesus Christ." Those words may be more true now than they ever were before. You say you believe in Jesus—act on your beliefs.

Here we are back on integrity again. If you believe that God leads you through your day, or that Jesus is your savior, act as though He is guiding your life. That does not mean you will never again make mistakes. It does mean that when you do make a mistake you pick y9urseof up and do your best to make things right, and you go on doing what God tells you is right.

There is the faith gained from paying really good attention to what is happening around us. Ralph Waldo Emerson once said tat for our love to benefit the world, we must first touch the world. Put your hands on what is in front of you. Feel how hard/soft/rough/scratchy this thing is. Feel it speak to you. Our sense of touch is marvelous and can be made so sensitive that we are able to feel the vibrations put out by every living thing. Through it we can sense the energy that flows through and from every living thing. If we are not alive to our sense of touch, we lose touch with reality, and when we lose touch with reality, we lose touch with God.

Touching the world. That's a good concept. Whose paths do we cross when we get out of bed in the morning? Who are the people we meet as we go about our day? They are our contact with the world. If our olove is to benefit the world, we must act with and interact with the people around us as God would have us act.

Throughout the Bible, touch is described as being powerful. From the first time touch is mentioned in the Book of Genesis, where Adam tells Eve not to touch the fruit of the tree of good and evil, for if she does she would surely die, to Genesis 32:25, when Jacob battles with the angel who has come down the ladder, the angel touches the hollow of Jacob's thigh, pushing it out of joint.

In Exodus, 29:37, God tells Moses, and Moses tells the Israelites, that whatever touches the altar within the holy tent, or mishkan, that they carry with them through the wilderness, shall also be holy.

Then we come to the healings in the New Testament. In Matthew 8:3, Jesus touches a man and says, Be thou clean. Immediately the man's sickness is removed. Throughout the first four books of the New Testament, Jesus touches many people, and people throng to touch him, because his touch heals them.

A kiss goes a long way towards healing a troubled spirit, and when the spirit is strong, the body heals itself much more easily. A back rub, or a message, stimulate not only circulation and relaxation to the troubled body, but remind us that we do not need to be alone.

Our world is filled with opposites; cold/hot, wet/dry; day/night. After sweating through a hot summer day, we welcome a cool shower in the evening, or a chance to splash in cold water at the swimming pool. After spending an hour or more shoveling snow in the middle of the winter, a warm kitchen and a good hot stew are very welcome indeed. We live through continuous cycles, like an ever deepening spiral, from day to night, summer to winter, round and round and back again. The tides in the ocean run through predictable cycles, lead by the cycles of the moon. The tide coming in would not be complete, nor would we appreciate it if it did not flow out again. The seasons flowing one into another and back again make this world a rich and varied place. The cycles of the moon, becoming round and full, and then all but completely disappearing in the night sky.